D0432091

50
economics
ideas
you really need to know

Edmund Conway

Quercus

Contents

Introduction

'A dreary, desolate and, indeed, quite abject and distressing [subject]; what we might call, by way of eminence, the dismal science.'

Thomas Carlyle's description of economics dates from 1849 but has stuck, for better or for worse. One should hardly be surprised. Economics is something people usually take notice of only when things go wrong. Only when an economy is facing a crisis, when thousands lose their jobs, when prices rise too high or fall too fast, do we tend to take much note of the subject. At such points there is little doubt it seems pretty dismal, especially when it underlines the challenges and the restraints we face, spells out the reality that we can't have everything we want and illustrates the fact that human beings are inherently imperfect.

The truth, I should add, in typical economist fashion, is far less simple. If it were merely a study of numbers, of statistics and of theories then the dismal science analogy would perhaps hold more ground. However, economics is, to its very heart, the study of people. It is an inquiry into how people succeed, into what makes us happy or content, into how humanity has managed over generations to become more healthy and prosperous than ever before.

Economics examines what drives human beings to do what they do, and looks at how they react when faced with difficulties or success. It investigates choices people make when given a limited set of options and how they trade them off against each other. It is a science that encompasses history, politics, psychology and, yes, the odd equation or two. If it is history's job to tell us what mistakes we've made over the past, it is up to economics to work out how to do things differently next time around.

Whether it succeeds in doing so is another question. As this book was going to press, the world was coming to terms with one of the biggest financial crises in history, as decades' worth of debt overwhelmed international markets. Some of the world's biggest and oldest banks, retailers and manufacturers collapsed. The crisis had many novel aspects – new and complex financial instruments, for example, and new economic relationships as, for the first time since the end of the Cold War, the position of the United States as global superpower came under question. But it was in reality very similar to many crises in the past. If we can make the same mistakes over and over again, went the cry, what is the purpose of economics?

The answer is very simple. The wisdom we have gleaned over centuries on how best to run our economies has made us richer, healthier and longer-lived than our forefathers could ever have contemplated. This is by no means a given. One has only to look at countries in sub-Saharan Africa and parts of Asia – where people are, in effect, stuck in the same conditions as Europe in the Middle Ages – to realize our prosperity is by no means assured. It is, in fact, extremely fragile, but as is always the case with economics, we take this success for granted and tend instead to focus on the dismal side of things.

Such is human nature. Many economics books attempt to dispel such illusions. This is rather desperate and, frankly, not my style. The aim of this book is simply to explain how the economy works. The dirty little secret of economics is that it's not really complicated at all – why should it be? It is the study of humanity, and as such its ideas are often little more than common sense.

This book is not intended to be read as a continuous narrative: each of these 50 ideas should make sense on its own, though I have highlighted where you might benefit from looking at another chapter.

My hope is that by the time you've read most of the ideas you will be able to think that little bit more like an economist: to ask probing questions about why we act the way we do; to reject the conventional wisdom; to understand that even the simplest things in life are more complicated than they seem – and all the more beautiful because of it.

A case in point is this Introduction. The done thing for an author is to include thanks to all who helped put the book together. But where to begin? Should I start by thanking the owners of the forest where the wood used to make the pages was felled? Or the factory workers who manufactured the ink that lines the pages? Or the operators of the machines in the bookbinding factory in China where the book was put together? Like so much else in this interconnected world, millions of people played a part in the creation of this book – from the publishers and manufacturers of the book you're holding, to the shipping firms that sailed it from China to your bookstore, alongside many others. (To find out why the book was printed in China, read the chapter on globalization.)

In particular, this book is a product of the thousands of conversations I have had with economists, professors, financiers, businessmen and politicians in recent years; and of the excellent economics literature available on store bookshelves and, more excitingly, the Internet. Many of the ideas echo those by prominent and less prominent economists too numerous to mention. However, I should like also to thank Judith Shipman at Quercus for allowing me to be part of this excellent series; my copy editors, Nick Fawcett and Ian Crofton; Vicki and Mark Garthwaite for giving me a place to write it; David Litterick, Harry Briggs and Olivia Hunt for their input; and my mother and the rest of my family for their support.

Edmund Conway, 2009

01 The invisible hand

'Greed is good,' declared Gordon Gekko, villain of the classic 1980s movie *Wall Street*, in one fell swoop confirming polite society's worst fears about financiers. In this cut-throat Manhattan world, flagrant avarice was no longer anything to be ashamed of – it should be worn with pride, like a striped shirt and red suspenders.

Shocking as the film was in the late 20th century, try to imagine how a declaration like that would have sounded some two centuries earlier, when intellectual life was still dominated by the Church, and defining humans as economic animals was close to blasphemous. Now you might have some idea of the impact Adam Smith's radical idea of the 'invisible hand' had when he first proposed it in the 18th century. Nevertheless, like its Hollywood descendant, his book was a massive commercial success, selling out on its first publishing run and remaining a part of the canon ever since.

The role of self-interest The 'invisible hand' is shorthand for the law of supply and demand (see chapter 2) and explains how the pull and push of these two factors serve to benefit society as a whole. The simple conceit is as follows: there is nothing wrong with people acting in their self-interest. In a free market, the combined force of everyone pursuing his or her own individual interests is to the benefit of society as a whole, enriching everyone.

Smith used the phrase only three times in his 1776 masterpiece *The Wealth of Nations*, but one key passage underlines its importance:

timeline

350BC	1723	1759
Aristotle declares that property should be private	Adam Smith born	*The Theory of Moral Sentiments* by Adam Smith is published

[Every individual] neither intends to promote the public interest, nor knows how much he is promoting it . . . by directing [his] industry in such a manner as its produce may be of the greatest value, he intends only his own gain, and he is in this, as in many other cases, led by an invisible hand to promote an end which was no part of his intention . . . By pursuing his own interest he frequently promotes that of the society more effectually than when he really intends to promote it. I have never known much good done by those who affected to trade for the public good.

The idea helps explain why free markets have been so important to the development of complex modern societies.

Taught by the hand Let's take an inventor, Thomas, who has come up with an idea for a new type of light bulb – one that is more efficient, longer-lasting and brighter than the rest. He has done so to serve his own self-interest, in the hope of making himself rich, and perhaps famous. The by-product will be to benefit society as a whole, by creating jobs for those who will make the bulbs and enhancing the lives (and living rooms) of those who buy them. If there had been no demand for the light bulb, no one would have paid Thomas for it, and the invisible hand would have, in effect, slapped him down for making such a mistake.

Similarly, once Thomas is in business, others may see him making money and attempt to outdo him by devising similar light bulbs that are brighter and better. They too start getting rich. However, the invisible hand never sleeps. Thomas starts undercutting his competitors so as to ensure he keeps selling the most. Delighted customers benefit from even cheaper light bulbs.

At each stage of the process Thomas would be acting in his own interests rather than for those of society, but, counter-intuitively, everyone would benefit as a result. In a sense, the theory of the invisible hand is analogous to the idea in mathematics that two negatives make a positive. If only one

1776

The Wealth of Nations by
Adam Smith is published

2007

Smith's contribution as the father
of economics is recognized on
the £20 banknote

ADAM SMITH 1723–90

The father of economics was a rather unlikely radical hero from the small Scottish town of Kirkcaldy. Fittingly for the first economist, Smith was an eccentric academic who considered himself an outsider, and occasionally bemoaned his unusual physical appearance and lack of social graces. Like many of his modern inheritors, his office at Glasgow University was stacked chaotically high with papers and books. Occasionally he was to be seen talking to himself, and he had a habit of sleepwalking.

Smith originally coined the phrase the 'invisible hand' in his first book, *The Theory of Moral Sentiments* (1759), which focused on how humans interact and communicate, and on the relationship between moral rectitude and man's innate pursuit of self-interest. After leaving Glasgow to tutor the young Duke of Buccleuch, he started work on the book that later became, to give it its full title, *An Inquiry into the Nature and Causes of the Wealth of Nations*.

Smith became something of a celebrity thereafter, and his ideas not only influenced all the big names of economics but also helped propel the Industrial Revolution and the first wave of globalization, which ended with the First World War. In the past 30 years, Smith has become a hero again, with his ideas on free markets, free trade and the division of labour (see chapter 6) underpinning modern economic thought.

Fittingly, in 2007, Smith was honoured as the first Scot to appear on a Bank of England banknote, with his face being displayed on the £20 note.

person is acting in his or her own self-interest, but everyone else is being altruistic, the benefits of society will not be served.

One example concerns Coca-Cola, which changed the recipe of its fizzy drink in the 1980s in an effort to attract younger, more fashionable drinkers. However, New Coke was a complete disaster: the public did not appreciate the change, and sales plunged. The message of the invisible hand was clear and Coca-Cola, its profits slumping, withdrew New Coke after a few months. The old variety was reinstated, and customers were happy – as were Coca-Cola's directors, since its profits quickly bounced back.

Smith recognized that there were circumstances under which the invisible hand theory would not work. Among them is a dilemma often known as the 'tragedy of the commons'. The problem is that when there is only a limited supply of a particular resource, such as grazing land on a common, those who exploit the land will do so to the detriment of their neighbours. It is an argument that has been used with great force by those who campaign against climate change (see chapter 45).

> **It is not from the benevolence of the butcher, the brewer or the baker that we expect our dinner, but from their regard to their own interest. We address ourselves, not to their humanity but to their self-love, and never talk to them of our own necessities but of their advantages.**
>
> **Adam Smith**

Limits to free markets

Although the idea of the invisible hand has occasionally been hijacked by right-wing politicians in recent decades, it is not a theory that necessarily represents a particular political view. It is a positive economic theory (see chapter 16), though it seriously undermines those who think economies can be run better from the top down, with governments deciding what ought to be produced.

The invisible hand underlines the fact that individuals – rather than governments and administrators – should be able to decide what to produce and consume, but there are some important provisos. Smith was careful to distinguish between self-interest and pure selfish greed. It is in our self-interest to have a framework of laws and regulations that protect us, as consumers, from being treated unfairly. This includes property rights, the enforcing of patents and copyrights and laws protecting workers. The invisible hand must be backed up by the rule of law.

This is where Gordon Gekko got it wrong. Someone driven purely by greed might choose to cheat the law in an effort to enrich himself to the detriment of others. Adam Smith would never have approved.

the condensed idea
Self-interest is good for society

02 Supply and demand

At the heart of economics and the very core of human relations lies the law of supply and demand. The way these two forces interact determines the prices of goods in the shops, the profits a company makes, and how one family becomes rich while another remains poor.

The law of supply and demand explains why supermarkets charge so much more for their premium sausages than their regular brand; why a computer company feels it can charge customers extra for a notebook computer merely by changing the colour. Just as a few elementary rules determine mathematics and physics, the simple interplay between supply and demand is to be found everywhere.

It is there in the crowded lanes of Otavalo in Ecuador and the wide avenues bordering Wall Street in New York. Despite their superficial differences – the dusty South American streets full of farmers, Manhattan replete with besuited bankers – in the eyes of the fundamentalist economist the two places are virtually identical. Look a little closer and you'll see why: they are both major markets. Otavalo is one of Latin America's biggest and most famous street markets; Wall Street, on the other hand, is home to the New York Stock Exchange. They are places where people go to buy or sell things.

The market brings the buyers and sellers together, whether at a physical set of stalls on which the products are sold or a virtual market such as Wall Street, where most trading is done through computer networks. And at the

timeline

1776	1807	1890
The Wealth of Nations by Adam Smith is published	French economist Jean-Baptiste Say lays down his law – that demand would always match supply over time	Alfred Marshall popularizes supply–demand curves and tables

nexus between demand and supply is the price. These three apparently innocuous pieces of information can tell us an immense amount about society. They are the bedrock of market economics.

Demand represents the amount of goods or services people are willing to buy from a vendor at a particular price. The higher the price, the less people will want to buy, up to the point when they simply refuse to buy at all. Similarly, supply indicates the amount of goods or services a seller will part with for a certain price. The lower the price, the fewer goods the vendor will want to sell, since making them costs money and time.

> **'We might as well reasonably dispute whether it is the upper or under blade of a pair of scissors that cuts a piece of paper, as whether value is governed by demand or supply.'**
>
> **Alfred Marshall,**
> **Victorian economist**

The price is right? Prices are the signal that tell us whether the supply of or demand for a particular product is rising or falling. Take house prices. In the early years of the 21st century they rose faster and faster in the US as more and more families took the plunge into home ownership, encouraged by cheap mortgage deals. This demand prompted housebuilders to construct more homes – particularly in Miami and parts of California. When, eventually, the homes were completed, the sudden glut of supply caused house prices to fall – and fast.

The open secret about economics is that, in reality, prices are rarely ever at their equilibrium. The price of roses rises and falls throughout the year: as summer turns to winter and supermarkets and florists have to source them from further abroad, the supply of roses drops and the price increases. Similarly, in the run-up to 14 February prices leap because of the demand for Valentine's Day flowers.

Economists term this 'seasonality' or 'noise'. Some, however, try to look beyond it to work out the equilibrium price. Take house prices again: no economist has yet worked out how much the average house should be worth. History tells us it should be worth a number of times someone's

1930s

Sir John Hicks refines the economics of supply and demand

Supply and demand in action

In Ecuador, Maria is selling fine, homespun colourful Andean-style blankets on her stall in the market. She knows there is no point in selling each blanket at $10 or less, since at that price she could not afford to make the blanket or rent the stall. First, then, she sets the price at $50, at which level she can afford to make 80 blankets, but this proves too expensive for prospective customers and none get sold, so she starts dropping the price in order to clear her stock. Slowly but surely demand builds up for the blankets. Each time she drops the price, more customers arrive. At $40 she gets 20 sales, at $30 she can shift 40 blankets. By the time she gets the price down to $20 she realizes she has set it too low. As her stocks deplete she realizes she is not making new blankets fast enough to keep up with demand. She realizes that at a price of $30 the number of blankets she was making was keeping pace with the number that people wanted. She has just plotted the most

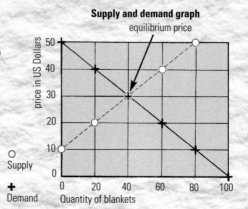

Supply and demand graph
equilibrium price

price in US Dollars

Quantity of blankets

○ Supply

+ Demand

important of all economic charts: a supply–demand curve. She has just discovered the equilibrium price for blankets.

The solid black line denotes the demand people have for Maria's blankets; the broken grey the supply. When blankets are priced at zero, there is demand for 100 of them, but there is no supply (since they cost more than that to manufacture). When they are priced at $20 there is potential demand for 60 but Maria can only make 20 of them. The equilibrium price for blankets, according to the chart, is 30 dollars. This is when supply equals demand – as the graph shows.

salary – between three or four times on average – but there is no way of knowing for sure.

One can learn some elementary lessons about people from the price of certain goods. A few years ago computer manufacturer Apple brought out its new Macbook laptop, and produced it in two colours, white and black, the second being a special, more expensive, version. Despite being identical in every other way to the white version – speed, hard disk space and so on – the black version was retailed for an extra $200. And yet they still sold successfully. This would not have happened without there being sufficient demand, so clearly people were happy to pay extra purely in order to distinguish themselves from their run-of-the-mill white laptop neighbours.

Elastic fantastic Sometimes supply and demand take a while to respond to changes in prices. If a telephone company raises its call charges, consumers tend to cut back pretty quickly on the number of calls they make or, alternatively, to move to a different phone company. In economic parlance, their demand is price *elastic* – it alters with changes in prices.

In other cases, consumers are slow to react to changes in costs – they are price *inelastic*. For example, when oil prices rose sharply early this millennium, consumers faced with high fuel prices could not switch to an alternative, nor could they necessarily afford to buy a new, expensive, electric or hybrid car to cut costs. Similarly, oil-intensive companies could do little but absorb the extra cost. Gradually, some consumers switched to using public transport. Such switches are known as substitution away from expensive items to alternatives. Many families, though, had little choice but to shoulder the higher cost of fuel for as long as possible.

> '**Teach a parrot the terms "supply and demand" and you've got an economist.**'
> **Thomas Carlyle**

Of course, what goes for demand goes equally for supply, which can also be elastic or inelastic. Many businesses have become extremely adaptive – or price elastic – when demand for their products drops, laying off workers or cutting back on investment as a response. Others, however, are more inelastic and therefore find things less easy. For instance, a Caribbean banana producer might find it extremely difficult to cut back on his business if he is either muscled out by bigger Latin American producers or finds that consumers are less keen to buy his bananas.

Whether it be the Ecuadorian stallholder, the Wall Street banker or anyone else, the primary force behind economic decisions is always the interplay between prices and the buyers and sellers who determine them; in other words, supply and demand.

the condensed idea
Something is perfectly priced when supply equals demand

03 The Malthusian trap

It is paradoxical that one of the most popular, powerful and enduring theories in economics has been proven wrong generation after generation. But then, there are few more captivating ideas than that the human race is expanding and exploiting the planet's resources so fast that it is heading for inevitable self-annihilation. Behold the Malthusian trap.

You are probably familiar from your biology lessons with those microscopic images of cells multiplying. You start with a couple of cells, each of which divide to form another pair; they multiply rapidly, second by second spreading out to the corners of the Petri dish until, eventually, they have filled it to its very edge and there is no more room left. What happens then?

Now take humans. They also reproduce at an exponential rate. Might we not be expanding too fast to be able to sustain ourselves? Two centuries ago, English economist Thomas Malthus was convinced we were. Humans were growing much faster than were their sources of food, he calculated. More specifically, he came up with the idea that the human population was rising geometrically (i.e. by multiples – 2, 4, 8, 16, 32 . . .) while the food available to them was growing arithmetically (i.e. by addition – 2, 4, 6, 8 . . .).

As Malthus himself said in his 1798 *Essay on the Principle of Population*, man needs food in order to survive, and man is multiplying at a rapid rate. He concluded:

timeline

1776

The Wealth of Nations by Adam Smith is published

I say that the power of population is indefinitely greater than the power in the earth to produce subsistence for man. Population, when unchecked, increases in a geometrical ratio. Subsistence only increases in an arithmetical ratio. A slight acquaintance with the numbers will show the immensity of the first power in comparison with the second.

In his eyes, the human race was heading for an inevitable crunch. Unless it voluntarily cut its birth rate (which he thought was inconceivable), the human population would suffer one of three unpalatable checks imposed by nature to keep it at certain sustainable limits: famine, disease or war. People would be unable to eat, succumb to some plague or another, or fight each other for increasingly scarce resources.

You can see why the Malthusian trap is often referred to as the Malthusian catastrophe or dilemma. This profound problem is still used today by various experts who advocate the necessity of controlling the size of the world population. It is an idea which has been adopted by many environmental movements to illustrate the unsustainability of the human race.

Problems with the theory But Malthus was wrong. Since he put pen to paper, the global population, which he thought was reaching a natural peak, has grown from 980 million to 6.5 billion. It is projected to balloon to more than 9 billion by 2050. Yet the majority of people on the planet are better fed, more healthy and longer-lived than ever before. Malthus was wrong in two areas:

> **❛Malthus has been buried many times, and Malthusian scarcity with him. But as Garrett Hardin remarked, anyone who has to be reburied so often cannot be entirely dead.❜**
> Herman E. Daly, US economist

1. Humans themselves have a track record in devising technologies to solve these problems. Partly thanks to the laws of supply and demand, which have encouraged producers to devise better, more efficient means of generating food, the world has seen a series of agricultural

1798	**1805**	**1859**
Essay on the Principle of Population by Thomas Robert Malthus is published	Malthus becomes professor of economics at Haileybury	*On the Origin of Species* by Charles Darwin – and influenced by Malthus's ideas – is published

THOMAS ROBERT MALTHUS 1766–1834

Despite being the man who inspired Thomas Carlyle's dismissal of economics as 'the dismal science', Thomas Malthus was in fact a highly popular, entertaining character, sociable and well regarded, despite his gloomy ideas. He was born into a wealthy family with an intellectual bent – indeed his father was an acquaintance of the philosophers David Hume and Jean-Jacques Rousseau – and spent most of his life either studying or teaching, bar a period as an Anglican curate. Economics was seen as so protean a subject that it was not recognized in its own right by most universities, so Malthus studied and later taught mathematics at Jesus College, Cambridge. However, it is a testament to the growing popularity of economics that in the early 19th century he became the world's first ever economics professor, teaching the subject at the East India Company College (now known as Haileybury) in Hertfordshire. And, in 1818, in a clear sign of the field's importance, Malthus became a Fellow of the Royal Society, in recognition of his pioneering work in economics.

revolutions, each dramatically increasing the available resources. Humans, with the help of the market, solved the food problem.

2. Population does not always grow exponentially. It has a natural tendency to level off after a period. Unlike cells, which will multiply until they have filled the dish, humans tend, once they reach a certain level of affluence, to reproduce less. In fact, human fertility has been dropping significantly recently, with birth rates in Japan, Canada, Brazil, Turkey and all of Europe insufficient to prevent depopulation. Longer life spans means the population is becoming gradually older, but that is another story (see chapter 32).

Economic historian Gregory Clark argues in his controversial book *A Farewell to Alms* that until 1790 man was indeed stuck in a Malthusian trap, but, due to a combination of factors thereafter – including the ill-fortune of the poorest to be killed off by disease, the need for them to be replaced by children of the upper and middle classes ('downward social mobility') and the proclivity of these classes to work harder – England escaped. He asserts that many parts of the world, having still not undergone this experience, remain stuck in the trap.

However, what was certainly not wrong was the theory underlying Malthusianism: *the law of diminishing returns*. It has important lessons for businesses. Take a small farm or factory. The boss decides to add one extra member of staff each week. To start with, each new employee causes a big jump in production. Some weeks later, though, there will come a point when each new worker makes that little bit less difference than the previous one. There is only so much difference an extra pair of hands can make when there is a finite number of fields or machines with which to work.

Apocalypse where? The way most of what we now call the Western world (Europe, the US, Japan and a handful of other advanced economies) broke out of the Malthusian trap was by raising agricultural productivity while at the same time, people as they grew wealthier had fewer children. This, alongside the invention of new technologies, helped fuel the Industrial Revolution, and eventually catapulted levels of wealth and health ever higher. Unfortunately, there are parts of the world which are still stuck in the trap.

In many sub-Saharan African countries, the land produces so little food that the vast majority of people have to work in subsistence farming. When they boost agricultural output by using new technologies to grow more crops, their populations balloon, and the famines that often follow in years of bad harvests keep the population from growing and becoming richer in the ensuing years.

Apocalypse when? Neo-Malthusians argue that although human ingenuity has managed to delay the catastrophe for a couple of centuries, we are now on the brink of another crunch. They contend that although Malthus's arguments revolved around food, one could just as easily insert oil and energy sources as being the chief 'means of man's support'. With the point of 'peak oil' close at hand, or perhaps having passed, the global population will soon reach unsustainable levels. Whether the technological advances or population restraint that prevented Malthus from being proved right hitherto will apply this time remains to be seen.

the condensed idea
Beware relentless rises in population

04 Opportunity cost

However wealthy and influential we may be, we can never find enough hours in the day to do everything we want. Economics deals with this problem through the notion of opportunity cost, which simply refers to whether someone's time or money could be better spent on something else.

Every hour of our time has a value. For every hour we work at one job we could quite easily be doing another, or be sleeping or watching a film. Each of these options has a different opportunity cost – namely, *what they cost us in missed opportunities*.

Say you intend to watch a football match but the tickets are expensive and it will take you a couple of hours to get to and from the stadium. Why not, you might reason, watch the game from home and use the leftover money and time (the time you'd have spent in pre- and post-match traffic) to have dinner with friends? This – the alternative use of your cash and time – is the opportunity cost.

Another example is whether or not to go to university. On the one hand, years spent there should be richly rewarding, both intellectually and socially; graduates also tend to receive better job opportunities. On the other hand, there is the cost of tuition, books and coursework. However, this ignores the opportunity cost: for the three or four years you are at university you could quite easily be in paid employment, earning cash and enhancing your CV with valuable work experience.

timeline

1776

The Wealth of Nations by Adam Smith is published

1798

Essay on the Principle of Population by Thomas Robert Malthus is published

> **'From the standpoint of society as a whole, the "cost" of anything is the value that it has in alternative uses.'**
>
> **Thomas Sowell, US economist**

Forgone opportunities The concept of opportunity cost is as important for businesses as for individuals. Take a shoe factory. The owner plans to invest £500,000 in a new machine that will dramatically speed up the rate at which he produces leather shoes. That money could just as easily be put into a bank account where it could earn 5 per cent interest a year. Therefore the opportunity cost of the investment is £25,000 a year – the amount forgone by investing in the machinery.

For economists, every decision is tempered by knowledge of what one must forgo – in terms of money and enjoyment – in order to take it up. By knowing precisely what you are receiving and what you are missing out on, you ought to be able to make better-informed, more rational decisions.

Consider that most famous economic rule of all: there's no such thing as a free lunch. Even if someone offers to take you out to lunch for free, with no expectation that you will return the favour or make conversation during the meal, the lunch is still not entirely free. The time you will spend in the restaurant still costs you something in terms of forgone opportunities.

Some people find the idea of opportunity cost immensely depressing: imagine spending your entire life calculating whether your time would be better spent elsewhere doing something more profitable or enjoyable. Yet, in a sense it's human nature to do precisely that – we assess the pros and cons of decisions all the time.

1817

Principles of Political Economy and Taxation by David Ricardo is published

1889

Friedrich von Wieser formalizes the concept of opportunity cost

Making money work for you

Most of us have experienced that sinking feeling when we've bet on the wrong team in a sports game or backed an investment that fails rather than making a million. That feeling is the realization of opportunity cost – of an opportunity missed. Consider the scenario of a pound invested in UK Treasury bills – a kind of government debt – in 1900. One hundred years later it was worth £140. A pound that had simply tracked inflation would have been worth just £54, but put it into UK equities – another word for shares – its value would have risen to £16,946. In this case the opportunity cost of failing to invest in shares was immense.

When it comes to buying a home, the opportunity costs are far more unpredictable. On the one hand, when house prices are rising fast, those who rent rather than buy may fear they are missing out on a possible money-spinner. However, they will be far better off when house prices are falling because they are immune from the impact. Just as importantly, when you put away a chunk of your income for a deposit, you are forgoing the possible gains you could make by investing that money elsewhere.

In the world of business, a popular slogan is 'value for money'. People, it is said, want their cash to go as far as possible. However, another slogan is fast gaining ground: 'value for time'. The biggest constraint on our resources is the number of hours we can devote to something, so we look to maximize the return we get on our investment of time. By reading this chapter you are giving over a small slice of your time which could be spent doing other activities – sleeping, eating, watching a film and so on. In return, however, this chapter will help you to think like an economist, closely considering the opportunity cost of each of your decisions.

Opportunity cost at home Whether we realize it or not, we all make judgements based on the idea of opportunity cost. If your pipes spout a leak at home, you could decide to fix the problem yourself, having worked out that even after you've paid for the tools, the book on plumbing and so forth you will still save a considerable sum compared with calling out a professional. However, the extra invisible cost is those things you might have done with the time spent undertaking the repair – not to mention the fact that a plumber would probably do a better job. Such an idea is closely tied in with the theory of comparative advantage (see chapter 7).

Opportunity cost in government Governments around the world similarly employ the opportunity cost argument when it comes to privatization. They reason not only that public utilities would often be better run in the private sector, but also that the money freed up from the sale could be used more effectively for public investment.

However, decisions taken with an eye on the opportunity cost can often go wrong. Back in 1999, British Chancellor Gordon Brown decided to sell off almost 400 tonnes – the vast majority – of the UK's gold reserves. At that point, the gold had been sitting idle in the Bank of England's vaults for many years, and its value had fallen, since many regarded gold as a poor investment. The same cash, had it been invested in securities such as government bonds, would have risen steadily in those previous years. So the UK Treasury decided to sell off the gold for an average price of $276 an ounce in exchange for various kinds of bonds.

> **'The cost of something is what you give up to get it.'**
> Greg Mankiw, Harvard economics professor

Few could have foreseen that less than a decade later, the price of gold had climbed sharply, to just below $981 per ounce, meaning that the gold Gordon Brown had sold off for $3.5 billion would now have been worth some $12.5 billion. The UK government made some profit from investing the proceeds of the sale – but not a fraction of what it would have made had it left the gold where it was sitting and sold it later. This illustrates one of the perils of opportunity cost – it encourages you to believe that the grass is always greener.

the condensed idea
Time is money

05 Incentives

For years it was one of the best-kept secrets in Jamaica. Coral Spring Beach was among the whitest and most glorious stretches of coast on the Caribbean island's north side. But then, one morning in 2008, developers building a hotel nearby arrived to discover something bizarre. The sand had gone. Thieves had been in under cover of night and stolen 500 truck-loads of the stuff.

Barrels of sand are more or less worthless in most parts of the world, but clearly not so in Jamaica. Who then committed the crime? Was it a rival in the tourist industry, who wanted the sand for their own beach; or was it a construction company planning to use it as a building material? Either way, one thing was clear: someone had taken desperate measures to get hold of the sand – someone with a serious incentive for doing so.

Rather like the detectives working on this case, an economist's job is, all too often, to work out what drives people to take certain decisions. He or she must detach themselves from the moral, political or sociological questions behind why people do things and must instead empirically determine the forces that push them towards their decisions.

Finding the motive A criminal robs a bank because he judges the incentive of taking its cash as greater than the disincentive of a spell in jail. A country's citizens work less hard when tax rates are increased, since the higher charges on their extra cash means they have less incentive to put in that extra hour. People respond to potential rewards. It is the most fundamental rule of economics.

timeline

1723	1798	1803
Adam Smith is born	*Essay on the Principle of Population* by Thomas Robert Malthus is published	Jean-Baptiste Say argues that there could never be a shortfall of demand in an economy

Think hard about why you and the people around you take certain decisions. A mechanic fixes your car not because you need to get back on the road again but because he is paid to do so. The waitress who serves you lunch does so for the same reason – not because you are hungry. And she does it with a smile not merely because she is a kindly person, but because restaurants depend heavily on repeat business to survive.

Although money plays an important part in economics, incentives do not merely apply to cash. Men and women spend that little bit longer dressing up for a date because of the incentive of romance. You might turn down a well-paid job that demands long hours in favour of a less generous salary because of the incentive of having more free time.

There are hidden incentives behind everything. For instance, most supermarket chains offer their customers reward cards, which give them occasional discounts off their shopping. The customer is given the incentive to shop more regularly with that outlet, which in turn guarantees the supermarket more sales.

> **'Call it what you will, incentives are what get people to work harder.'**
> **Nikita Khrushchev**

However, another important incentive for the supermarket is the fact that the card enables it to track closely what certain customers are buying. As a result it not only has a far better idea about what to stock on its shelves, but can entice customers with customized special offers and make some extra cash by selling details of the shopper's purchasing habits to external marketing agents, for whom such information is highly valuable. Because of the invisible hand (see chapter 1) both parties in the equation benefit, having along each step of the way responded to strong incentives.

Controversial as it is, one can even frame apparently altruistic acts as rational economic decisions. To what extent do people give to charity because of inherent kindness or because of the emotional reward (the contentedness and sense of duty done) that it endows? The same could be

1817	1871	1890
Principles of Political Economy and Taxation by David Ricardo is published	Carl Menger first states basic principle of marginal utility, revolutionizing study of incentives	*Principles of Economics* by Alfred Marshall is published

Healthy incentives

The realization that incentives matter sparked a novel approach to tackling the spread of AIDS in Africa. Having tried and failed to quell the spread of the disease by handing out condoms and educating the people of Africa about the dangers of sexually transmitted diseases, the World Bank did something unusual. It agreed to pay 3,000 men and women from Tanzania from a fund of $1.8 million to avoid unsafe sex; to prove that they had done so they had to take regular tests to show they had not contracted any sexual diseases. It called the scheme 'reverse prostitution'.

These so-called 'conditional cash transfers' have been used to great effect in Latin America to encourage poor parents to visit health clinics, and to have their children vaccinated and schooled. They are usually cheaper than other measures.

said of organ donors. Although behavioural economics has uncovered clear examples of humans responding in unexpected ways to rewards (see chapter 46), the vast majority of decisions can be traced back to a simple combination of incentives.

Despite the fact that these incentives are not always financial, economists usually focus on money – rather than love or fame – because cash is easier to quantify than self-esteem or happiness.

Government and incentives In times of economic hardship, governments often cut their citizens' taxes – as they did during the recession that followed the 2008 financial crisis. The aim is to give people an incentive to carry on spending, and therefore to lessen the scale of the economic slowdown.

But people respond as much to the stick as to the carrot, so governments often use disincentives to ensure their citizens conform to certain norms. Clear examples include the fines levied for parking or traffic offences. Other examples include so-called 'sin taxes' – extra levies on harmful items such as cigarettes and alcohol – and environmental taxes on petrol, emissions of waste products, and so forth. Ironically, such taxes are among the biggest revenue generators for governments around the world.

Incentives and disincentives are so powerful that history is littered with examples of governments causing major crises by attempting to prevent the push and pull of self-interest.

There have been numerous instances where food prices have rocketed and governments have hit back by imposing controls on them. The ostensible idea is to get more food to the poorest families, but such policies have repeatedly failed – in fact, more often than not they result in even less food being produced. Because price controls undermine farmers' incentives to produce food, either they give up their jobs or they tend to produce less and hold back what they can for their own families.

In the most egregious recent example, President Richard Nixon, much against his own instincts and those of his advisers, imposed price and wage controls in 1971. The end result was major economic hardship and, ultimately, increased inflation. However, the Nixon administration had a clear incentive for imposing the controls: it was facing an election, and knew that the disagreeable effects of the policy would take some time to become apparent. In the short run, the plan was immensely popular with the public – and Nixon was re-elected in November 1972 with a landslide.

Another example was the experience of the Soviet Union during communism. Because central planners enforced price controls on food, farmers had little incentive to plough even their most fertile fields; meanwhile millions starved to death throughout the country.

The lesson from such examples is that self-interest is the most powerful force in economics. Through the course of our lives we are drawn from one incentive to another. To ignore this is to ignore the very fabric of human nature.

the condensed idea
People respond to incentives

06 Division of labour

The Spaniard looked up at the magnificent scene in front of him and gasped in amazement. The year was 1436 and he was in Venice to see how the Italian city state armed its warships. Back home, this was a laborious process taking days, but here before his very eyes the Venetians were arming ship after ship in less than an hour a go. But how exactly did they do it?

Back in Spain, ships had to be tied up at the dock as hordes of workers loaded the vessel with fresh munitions and supplies. In Venice, by contrast, each ship was towed down a canal, and the different specialist weapon producers lowered their products onto its deck as it passed by. Mouth gaping, the Spanish tourist recorded the process in his diary. He had just witnessed the apotheosis of the division of labour: one of the world's first production lines.

The idea is simply this: we can produce far more, far better, by dividing up the work and specializing in what each of us is good at. Division of labour has been practised for millennia. It was already well established in Greek times; it was in place in factories around the country in Adam Smith's day, but it took until the early 20th century for it to meet its culmination in the shape of Henry Ford and his Model-T car.

Division of labour is what helped drive the first Industrial Revolution, enabling countries around the world to improve their productivity and

timeline

360 BC	1430
Plato cites specialism in his *Republic*	The arsenal of Venice – standardized parts and assembly-line techniques

Division on a big scale

Dividing up labour makes sense, whether on a small or large scale. For instance, take a region that is particularly suited for farming wheat, having the right soil density and rainfall levels, but that frequently has to let parts of its land lie fallow since its inhabitants cannot cut enough of the wheat at harvest time. Residents of the neighbouring region are expert at making blades for swords and tools, but its land is pretty barren and its inhabitants often have to go hungry.

The powerful logic of division of labour says that the two regions should specialize in what they are good at and import what they struggle to produce. The inhabitants of each would then have sufficient food and as many blades as they need either to harvest the wheat or to protect themselves.

wealth dramatically. It is the production method behind almost every manufactured object you care to think of.

The complexity of manufacture Take a regular lead pencil. Its creation involves a multiplicity of different steps: chopping the wood, mining and shaping the graphite, adding the labelling, the lacquer and the eraser. It took countless hands to manufacture one single pencil, as Leonard Read, founder of the Foundation for Economic Education, wrote in his inspiring short work *I, Pencil* (1958): 'Simple? Yet, not a single person on the face of this earth knows how to make me. This sounds fantastic, doesn't it? Especially when it is realized that there are about one and one-half billion of my kind produced in the USA each year.'

Not until the era of Adam Smith was division of labour summed up in a simple theory. The famous example Smith used in *The Wealth of Nations*

1776

Adam Smith explains how division of labour works, by describing the process in a pin factory

1913

Henry Ford and the assembly line – automation of car manufacture

> **'Where the whole man is involved there is no work. Work begins with the division of labour.'**
>
> Marshall McLuhan, Canadian media theorist

was that of a pin factory in 18th-century Britain, where small pins were manufactured by hand. The average man on the street could scarcely make a pin a day, he said, but in a pin factory the work was divided among a number of specialists:

> One man draws out the wire, another straights it, a third cuts it, a fourth points it, a fifth grinds it at the top for receiving the head; to make the head requires two or three distinct operations . . . the important business of making a pin is, in this manner, divided into about eighteen distinct operations.

According to Smith, one factory of 10 men could produce 48,000 pins a day by dividing up the labour – a stupendous 400,000 per cent increase in productivity. Working in this way the team produces considerably more than the sum of their parts.

This is, of course, the prototype for the kind of factory created by Henry Ford a century ago. He devised a moving production line whereby the car being constructed would pass on a conveyor belt in front of different teams of workers, each of which would add a new – standardized – part to it. The result was that he could produce a car for a fraction of the price, and in a fraction of the time, that it took his competitors.

Sticking to one's strengths However, division of labour does not stop there. Consider a company where the managing director is far better than his employees at administration, management, accounting, marketing and cleaning the building. He would be far better served delegating all but one of these tasks to his employees, and taking for himself the most profitable one.

In a similar vein, it makes no sense for a car manufacturer to make every single part of its vehicles, from the leather on the seats to the engine to the sound system. It is better off leaving some, or all, of these specialist processes to other companies, buying the products off them and simply assembling them.

Smith took the idea one step further: he suggested labour should be divided up not only between different individuals suited to certain tasks, but also between different cities and countries.

The dangers of division There are, however, problems inherent with dividing up labour. The first is that, as anyone made redundant will testify, it can be extraordinarily difficult to find work when you specialize in a craft that is no longer in demand. Hundreds of thousands of car workers, coal miners, steel workers and so on have, in recent decades, found themselves consigned to long-term unemployment after the factories, plants and mines they worked in shut down. Second, a factory can become entirely dependent on one person, or a small group of people, which can allow them to wield disproportionate power over the entire process – going out on strike, for instance, should they have a grievance.

Third, it can be dangerously morale-sapping for an individual to be forced to specialize only in one specific trade or expertise. Having to carry out a single repetitive job each day leads to what Smith called a 'mental mutilation' in workers, degrading their minds and alienating them from others. It was an analysis with which Karl Marx heartily agreed. In fact, it forms part of the basis for his *Communist Manifesto*, which forecast that workers would become so disenchanted that they would eventually rise up against employers who imposed such conditions on them.

Nevertheless, the alienation engendered by the division of labour has to be set against the phenomenal gains it generates. The division of labour has informed the growth and development of modern economies to such an extent that it remains one of the most important and powerful pieces of economic logic.

the condensed idea
Concentrate on your specialities

07 Comparative advantage

If market economics had to be distilled into two key articles of faith they would be as follows: firstly, the invisible hand will mean that even self-interested acts will, en masse, be beneficial for society (see chapter 1); secondly, economic growth is not a zero-sum game, where for every winner there is a loser. These credos are counterintuitive – the latter in particular. It is human nature to assume that when someone gets richer or fatter or healthier it is at the expense of someone else in the world getting poorer, thinner or sicker.

Take two countries, for example Portugal and England. Say they trade two goods with each other – wine and cloth – and it so happens Portugal is more efficient than England at making both. It can produce cloth for half the price that England can and wine for a fifth of the price.

Portugal has what economists call an *absolute advantage* in producing both kinds of goods. On the face of it, the rule of division of labour – that one should specialize in what one is good at – doesn't seem to provide a solution. You might assume there is little England can do to compete, and it must resign itself to slowly losing its wealth. Not so.

In this case, if England devoted all its resources to producing cloth and Portugal likewise concentrated on wine, they would, together, end up producing more cloth and wine. Portugal could then trade its excess wine in exchange for English cloth. This is because, in our example, England

timeline

1776	1798
The Wealth of Nations by Adam Smith is published	*Essay on the Principle of Population* by Thomas Robert Malthus is published

has a *comparative advantage* in making cloth, as opposed to wine, where it is so much less efficient than the Portuguese. The father of comparative advantage, economist David Ricardo, used this example in his

Comparative advantage at work

Let's take two equal-sized countries, A and B. They trade shoes and corn, and country A is more efficient at making both. However, while country A can produce 80 bushels of corn per man hour compared with B's 30, it can only produce 25 shoes per man hour compared with B's 20. Country B therefore has a comparative advantage in shoe manufacture. This is what would happen if each country tried to produce both products:

	Country A man hours	A output	Country B man hours	B output
Corn	600	48,000 (600x80)	600	18,000
Shoes	400	10,000 (400x25)	400	8,000

Combined output = 66,000 bushels of corn and 18,000 shoes

However, if country A concentrated on producing corn and B on producing shoes, this is what would happen:

	Country A man hours	A output	Country B man hours	B output
Corn	1,000	80,000	0	
Shoes	0		1,000	20,000

Combined output = 80,000 bushels of corn and 20,000 shoes

Neither country is working any extra hours, but by concentrating on their comparative advantage, the two countries can, together, produce significantly more, and each will become better off.

The only circumstance under which comparative advantage would not work is if one country is not only more efficient than another at producing two types of goods but also more efficient in exactly the same proportion for each. In practice, this is so unlikely as to be effectively impossible.

1817

David Ricardo sets out comparative advantage in *On the Principles of Political Economy and Taxation*

1945

Push for freer trade begins after the Second World War

> **❛Name me one proposition in all of the social sciences which is both true and non-trivial.❜**
> **Stanislaw Ulam, mathematician**

groundbreaking 1817 book *On the Principles of Political Economy and Taxation*. It seems illogical at first because we are used to the idea that there can only be winners and losers when people are competing with each other. However, the law of comparative advantage shows that when countries trade with each other it can lead to a win-win result.

The reason is that each country only has a finite number of people, who can devote only a finite number of hours to a particular task. Even if Portugal could in theory produce something more cheaply than England it could not produce everything more cheaply since the time it spends making cloth, for example, comes at the expense of the time that could have been devoted to producing wine, or anything else for that matter.

Although comparative advantage is most often applied to international economics, it is just as important on a smaller scale. In the chapter on division of labour (see chapter 6) we imagined a businessman who was more talented than his staff at everything from management to keeping the building clean. We can use comparative advantage to explain why he is better off devoting his time to what generates the most cash (management) and leaving the other, less profitable tasks to his employees.

Always free trade? Ricardo's theory of comparative advantage is typically used as the backbone of arguments in favour of free trade – in other words abolishing tariffs and quotas on goods imported from foreign countries. It is claimed that, by trading freely with other countries – even those that, on paper, are more efficient at producing goods and services – one can become more prosperous than by closing one's borders.

However, some – including Hillary Clinton and prominent economist Paul Samuelson – have warned that, elegant as they are, Ricardo's ideas are no longer strictly applicable to today's rather more sophisticated economic world. In particular, they point out that when Ricardo set out his theory in the early 19th century there were effective restrictions on people moving their capital (their cash and assets) overseas. This is not the case today, when with one tap of a keyboard a businessman can transfer billions of dollars' worth of assets electronically from one side of the world to another.

Former General Electric chief executive Jack Welch used to talk about having 'every plant you own on a barge' – indicating that, ideally, factories should be able to float to wherever the costs of people, materials and taxation are lowest. Today such a scenario is arguably a reality, as companies, no longer tied to particular nations as they tended to be in Ricardo's day, shift their workers and cash to wherever they prefer. In effect, say some economists, this causes wages to fall rapidly and the citizens of some countries to end up worse off than others. The counter-argument is that, in return, the country which has hived off jobs overseas benefits from the higher profits of that company, which are redistributed to its investors, and from lower prices in the shops.

> 'Comparative advantage. That it is logically true need not be argued before a mathematician; that it is not trivial is attested by the thousands of important and intelligent men who have never been able to grasp the doctrine for themselves or to believe it after it was explained to them.'
>
> Paul Samuelson, US economist, in response to mathematician Stanislaw Ulam

Others argue that comparative advantage is too simplistic a theory, assuming, among other things, that each market is perfectly competitive (in reality, internal protectionism and monopolies ensure that markets are not), that there is full employment, and that displaced workers can easily move to other jobs at which they can be just as productive. Some complain that were economies to specialize in particular industries, as the theory of comparative advantage suggests, this would reduce their economic diversity significantly, leaving them highly vulnerable to a change in circumstances – for instance a sudden fall in consumers' appetite for their products. In Ethiopia, where coffee constitutes 60 per cent of exports, a change in demand from overseas, or a poor harvest, would leave the country in a weaker economic position.

Nevertheless, most economists argue that comparative advantage is still one of the most important and fundamental economic ideas of all, for it underlies world trade and globalization, proving that nations can prosper even more by looking outwards rather than inwards.

the condensed idea
Specialization + free trade = win-win

08 Capitalism

For Francis Fukuyama it was the moment that marked the 'End of History'. For millions in Eastern Europe and beyond it heralded a greater freedom and prosperity than they had ever before experienced. For David Hasselhoff it was the crowning concert of a hearteningly brief music career. The fall of the Berlin Wall meant a lot of things to a lot of people.

But most important of all was what that moment said about the way economies are structured and run. To most observers, the collapse of the Soviet Union proved incontrovertibly that market economies are the best way to run a country, to make it prosperous and to keep its citizens happy. It was a victory for capitalism.

Capitalism has attracted perhaps more criticism than any other model of economics – indeed, its name was originally a term of disparagement devised by socialists and Marxists in the 19th century to refer to the most objectionable aspects of modern economic life – exploitation, inequality and suppression to name just three. In its early days the model came under fire from the Church since its prioritization of profit and money was regarded as a threat to religious teaching. The more enduring criticisms are that it generates inequality, promotes unemployment and instability, and has a tendency towards boom and bust. Others warn that it makes no allowance for its effect on the environment (see chapter 46).

A mongrel system Capitalism is the system where capital (the companies, equipment and structures used for producing goods and services) is owned not by the state but by private individuals. This means it is the public who own companies – taking stakes in them by buying

timeline

1000s	1500s
Feudalism takes hold	Mercantilism becomes dominant

shares, or by lending them money in exchange for bonds. Sometimes people do this directly; more often others invest on their behalf through pension funds. Almost every citizen of a major economy unwittingly owns shares in its major companies through his or her pension fund, meaning in theory that everyone has an interest in seeing business thrive.

Most economics textbooks don't actually bother to define capitalism. This is perhaps understandable. Unlike pure, relatively one-dimensional economic systems such as communism, capitalism is a mongrel. Complex and multifaceted, it steals from many other systems, and it is extremely difficult to pin down a precise definition. Not only that, but – as the economic system most countries in the world live by – it often seems gratuitous to try to define it.

Since it is people rather than governments who dominate the economy, capitalism usually goes hand in hand with the free market. But beyond this, a capitalist economy can take on many different guises.

Monopolies and other problems

Critics of capitalism have warned that it often has a proclivity towards *monopolies* (where one company takes exclusive control of an industry), *oligopolies* (where a group of companies share an effective monopoly) and *oligarchies* (where economies are run by small groups of powerful people). This is in contrast to perfect competition, where buyers always have plenty of alternative products to buy and companies have to compete with each other to win custom.

Monopolies are one of the big obstacles to a fully healthy economy, and governments spend much time attempting to ensure companies neither collaborate in cartels nor become so large that they dominate an entire industry. The problem is that monopolies are able to charge their customers more than they would if there was competition. This discourages them from taking the tough decisions to cut costs and become more efficient, which in turn undermines the law of creative destruction (see chapter 36).

In practice, what we tend to call capitalist economies these days – such as those of the United States, Britain and other European countries and many parts of the developing world – are better described as 'mixed economies', which combine the free market with government intervention. Fully free economies – often called laissez-faire, from the French for 'let (them) do

1800s
Industrial Revolution ushers in age of capitalism

1989
Fall of the Berlin Wall, triggering the spread of capitalism throughout the former communist world

(as they choose)' – have never existed. In fact, most leading nations are actually slightly less free market than they were a few centuries ago, as the history of the idea shows.

The evolution of capitalism Capitalism in its earliest form evolved as the *feudal* system in medieval Europe – in which agricultural labourers had to work for the profit of the landed gentry. This gave way in the late 16th century to *mercantilism*. This was a recognizable though crude precursor to capitalism, fuelled by trade between different nations and by the discovery by Europeans of lucrative resources in the Americas. The operators of these trade routes became extremely wealthy, and for the first time in history ordinary people started making money in their own right, rather than relying on the patronage of a rich monarch or aristocrat.

This was a critical epiphany, and although Adam Smith had plenty of issues with the finer points of mercantilism, its driving force – that individuals can profit through trade with each other – is one of the key precepts of the capitalism he espoused in *The Wealth of Nations*. Traders were far more cosseted by the state then than now, allowed to operate monopolies, and aided by government-imposed tariffs on imports. However, the legal structures that evolved over a 200-year period – private ownership, joint-stock companies – and the economic precepts of profit and competition were the foundations for modern-day capitalism.

> **'The inherent vice of capitalism is the unequal sharing of blessings; the inherent virtue of socialism is the equal sharing of miseries.'**
>
> **Winston Churchill**

In the 19th century merchants were replaced as the leading wealth generators by industrialists and factory owners, in what many regard as a golden age for free markets. In the US and the UK there were fewer constraints on markets and trade, and less government intervention, than there are in these countries today. However, the tendency of some industries to generate monopolies, and the economic and social trauma of the Great Depression in the 1930s – followed by the Second World War – spurred governments to intervene in their economies more, nationalizing certain select sectors and creating a welfare state for their citizens. Just before the Wall Street Crash in 1929, US government spending accounted for less than one-tenth of the country's economic output. Forty years later it accounted for around one-third. Today, it accounts for around 36 per cent, with that proportion fast on the rise. To understand precisely why there was such a jump, look no further than the next chapter in this book, which addresses Keynesianism. The story of capitalism over the past century has essentially revolved around this question of how much governments should spend and interfere in economies.

Capitalism and democracy The capitalist system has important implications for politics and freedom. Capitalism is inherently democratic. By allowing the invisible hand to function, by encouraging entrepreneurs to work hard and improve themselves, by prioritizing individuals' self-interest over the state's decisions about what might be best for people, and by allowing shareholders control over companies, it enshrines individual democratic and voting rights in society in a way other top-down systems simply can't do. It is no coincidence that non-capitalist societies have tended almost exclusively to be unelected dictatorships. However, in the case of modern China, many predict that the country's adoption of free-market values will eventually usher in a move towards democracy.

> ‘History suggests that capitalism is a necessary condition for political freedom.’
>
> **Milton Friedman**

Just as there is a constant tension in democratic societies between state interference and the rights of the individual, there is an important debate constantly raging about the extent to which capitalism treats some citizens unfairly while allowing others to prosper disproportionately. However, it is hard to find an economist who disagrees with the contention that, under capitalist systems, economies have become richer and healthier, developed faster, created more sophisticated technologies and generally had more serene political existences than under alternative systems. When the Berlin Wall and the Soviet Union fell it became clear to all that capitalism had left the Western economies in a far healthier position than those previously run under communism. Economist after economist has therefore concluded that, despite its many flaws, capitalism remains the best means we have yet discovered of running a modern, thriving economy.

the condensed idea
The least worst way to run an economy

09 Keynesianism

At the core of Keynesian economics is the idea that fiscal policy (government taxing and spending) should be used as a tool to control an economy. It was a theory espoused by one of the 20th century's greatest thinkers, British economist John Maynard Keynes, whose ideas helped shape the modern world economy and are still widely respected and followed today.

Keynes's magnum opus – *The General Theory of Employment, Interest and Money* (1936) – was a direct response to the Great Depression. He argued that governments had a duty, one that had hitherto been neglected, to help keep the economy afloat in times of trauma. It was a rebuke to an idea set out by Frenchman Jean-Baptiste Say (1767–1832) that throughout the economy as a whole 'supply creates its own demand', meaning that merely producing goods would spark demand for them.

Kick-starting the economy The assumption until the Great Depression had been that the economy was in large part self-regulated – that the invisible hand (see chapter 1), left to its own devices, would automatically raise employment and economic output to optimal levels. Keynes strongly disagreed. During a downturn, he said, the drop in demand for goods could cause a serious slump, causing the economy to contract and pushing up unemployment. It was the responsibility of government to kick-start the economy by borrowing cash and spending it, hiring public-sector staff and pouring cash into public infrastructure projects – for example, building roads and railways, hospitals and schools. Interest-rate cuts can go some way towards boosting an economy (see chapter 18), but they are not the whole answer.

timeline

1929	1933	1936
The Wall Street Crash sends stocks plunging and triggers the Great Depression	Franklin D. Roosevelt announces his New Deal – a programme of government works to try to arrest the Depression	Keynes argues in *The General Theory of Employment, Interest and Money* that governments should borrow more in times of recession

JOHN MAYNARD KEYNES 1883–1946

John Maynard Keynes was one of those rare things: an economist who also had the opportunity to put his theories into action. Called Maynard by his friends, he was a celebrated intellectual during his lifetime, and became part of the Bloomsbury Group, which also included Virginia Woolf and E.M. Forster. In the First World War he worked as adviser to the Chancellor of the Exchequer, but it was after the war that he really made his name. With some prescience, he warned that the harsh terms of the Versailles Treaty might lead to hyperinflation in Germany, and potentially another great war. History, of course, bore him out.

Keynes made a fortune on the stock market, though he lost much of it in the Great Crash of 1929, and had mixed fortunes speculating on currencies.

Before his death just after the Second World War, Keynes negotiated an essential loan from the United States, and helped design the International Monetary Fund and World Bank – the two major international economic institutions that shaped the world economy in the following decades.

According to Keynes, the extra cash spent by government would filter through the economy. For example, building a new motorway creates work for construction firms, whose employees go out and spend their money on food, goods and services, which in turn helps keep the wider economy ticking over. Key to his argument was the idea of the multiplier.

Say the United States government orders a $10 billion aircraft carrier from the shipbuilders Northrop Grumman. You might assume the effect of this would be merely to pump $10 billion into the economy. Under the multiplier argument, the actual effect would be bigger. Northrop Grumman takes on more employees and generates more profits; its workers spend more on consumer goods. Depending on the average consumer's 'propensity to consume', this could raise total economic output by far more than the amount of public money actually injected.

1970s

Keynesianism falls out of favour as Western nations battle against inflation

2008

Keynesian ideas return as governments across the world borrow and spend in order to fight recession

> **We really are all Keynesians now. A very large part of what modern macroeconomists do derives directly from *The General Theory*; the framework Keynes introduced holds up very well to this day.**
> **Paul Krugman, US economist**

If the $10 billion increase caused total United States economic output to rise by $5 billion, the multiplier would be 0.5; if it rose by $15 billion, the multiplier would be 1.5.

The six principal tenets According to former presidential adviser Alan Blinder, there are six principal tenets behind Keynesianism:

1. Keynesians believe that an economy's performance is influenced by both public and private decisions and sometimes behaves erratically.
2. The short term matters – sometimes even more than the long term. Short-term rises in unemployment may cause even more damage in the long run since they can leave a permanent dent in a country's economy. As Keynes famously said: 'In the long run, we are all dead.'
3. Prices and, especially, wages respond slowly to changes in supply and demand, which in turn means unemployment is often higher or lower than it ought to be given the economy's strength.
4. Unemployment is often too high and volatile, while recessions and depressions are economic maladies – not, as the invisible hand would have it, efficient market responses to unattractive opportunities.
5. The natural boom and bust of the economy is a problem that governments should actively attempt to stabilize.
6. Keynesians tend to be more concerned about combating unemployment than conquering inflation.

A controversial theory Keynesianism has always been controversial. On what basis, ask many of its critics, should we assume that governments know best how to run an economy? Is economic volatility really such a dangerous facet? Despite this, Keynes's arguments appeared to provide a solution to the Great Depression in the 1930s, and Franklin D. Roosevelt's New Deal – unveiled in response to the crisis – is seen as a classic example of a government 'priming the pump' of its economy by spending billions amid a recession. Arguments still rage over whether it was this or the Second World War that eventually brought the Depression to an end, but the powerful message was that government spending worked.

In the wake of *The General Theory*, governments around the world dramatically increased their levels of public spending, partly for social reasons – to set up welfare states to deal with the consequences of high unemployment – and partly because Keynesian economics underlined the importance of governments having control of significant chunks of the economy.

For a considerable time it seemed to work, with inflation and unemployment relatively low and economic expansion strong, but in the 1970s Keynesian policies came under fire, particularly from monetarists (see chapter 10). One of their main arguments was that governments cannot 'fine-tune' an economy by regularly adjusting fiscal and monetary policy to keep employment high. There is simply too long a time lag between recognizing the need for such a policy (tax cuts, say) and the policy actually taking effect – even if policymakers speedily identify the problem it takes time for laws to be drafted and passed, and more time still for the tax cuts to drip through the wider economy. By the time that tax cuts are actually having an effect, the problem they were designed to solve may have worsened – or dissipated.

Ironically, however, Keynes enjoyed a major comeback in the wake of the 2008 financial crisis. As it became clear that cuts in interest rates would not be enough to prevent the US, UK and other economies falling into a recession, economists argued that governments should borrow money in order to cut taxes and boost spending. That is precisely what they did, in what was widely seen as a serious break with the previous two and a half decades. Against all odds, Keynes was back.

the condensed idea
Governments should spend to prevent deep recessions

10 Monetarism

John Maynard Keynes versus Milton Friedman: the economics clash to end them all. It is not merely that the pair were both phenomenally intelligent, frequently caustic debaters; nor is it that they hail from such different backgrounds, the one an Eton-educated Englishman, the other the Brooklyn-born son of Hungarian Jewish immigrants. The fact is that the two men stood for radically opposing doctrines. They represent the ideological battle underlying the economics of the past 50 years.

Whereas Keynes paid more attention to unemployment than inflation, and warned that the economy could be improved by a certain amount of state interference, Friedman argued people should be left to their own devices with the government's main role to monitor and control the amount of money flowing around the economy. In his seminal book *A Monetary History of the United States 1867–1960*, co-authored with Anna Schwartz, he set out the theories of monetarism.

Always fight inflation 'Inflation is always and everywhere a monetary phenomenon,' Friedman said. In short, by pumping extra money into the system (as the Keynesians were prone to doing) governments would drive up inflation, risking major pain for the economy. Friedman believed that if central banks were charged with maintaining control of prices, most other aspects of the economy – unemployment, economic growth, productivity – would more or less take care of themselves.

While Keynes had asserted that it was highly difficult to persuade workers to accept lower wages, classical monetarist theory argued otherwise: that lower incomes for workers and lower prices for firms were acceptable in the

timeline

MILTON FRIEDMAN 1912–2006

Milton Friedman was one of the most influential thinkers in modern economics. He was born to a poor family of Hungarian Jewish immigrants in Brooklyn, New York, and at school he soon showed himself to be a bright student. After studying at Rutgers University, he undertook graduate work at Chicago University, which, under his influence, soon became one of the world's leading academic economics forums. During the Second World War he worked for the Federal Government, at one point advocating Keynesian-style government-spending policies. It was in the 1960s that his ideas on monetarism came to real prominence, and in 1976 he was awarded the Nobel Prize for Economics.

face of rising inflation. The growth rate of an economy, argued Friedman, could be determined by controlling the amount of money being printed by central banks. Print more cash and people would spend more, and vice versa. It was a far cry from Keynesianism, which downplayed the importance of money. It also marked an important political departure: whereas Keynes argued politicians should attempt to control the economy through fiscal policy, Friedman advocated giving independent central banks control over the economy using interest rates (albeit with some strict rules).

In a downturn, Friedman said, central banks should prevent deflation by pumping more money into the system. On this reasoning, he argued that in the run-up to the Great Depression, the Federal Reserve made the mistake of clamping down too hard on America's banks and allowing too many to fail, which in turn made the economic slump even more painful. In fact, he blamed the Fed for turning what might have been a minor recession into the depression it ultimately was.

An idea whose time had come At first the establishment paid little attention to Friedman's arguments, which were presented alongside a whole smorgasbord of radical free-market proposals, including making military service voluntary, allowing exchange rates to float freely, introducing educational vouchers, privatizing social security and instituting a negative income tax. After all, during the 1960s Keynesianism seemed to be working well: growth was steady, inflation was low and unemployment was under control. Who was this young economist arguing that the policies could potentially drive up inflation and unemployment – something that the Phillips Curve said was almost impossible (see chapter 22)?

> **'Friedman's monetary framework has been so influential that in its broad outlines at least, it has nearly become identical with modern monetary theory.'**
>
> **Ben Bernanke**

Then came the oil shocks and the economic turmoil of the 1970s. The Western world endured stagflation, with shrinking economic growth, rising inflation and joblessness. Keynesian economics seemed to have no answer for this, paving the way for Friedman's theory. He had predicted that such an outcome was possible and he proposed a solution: fight inflation, not unemployment.

On both sides of the Atlantic, politicians slowly embraced the doctrine. In the 1980s Paul Volcker, chairman of the Federal Reserve, took the United States through a painful and traumatic recession in order to get prices back under control. In the UK, incoming Prime Minister Margaret Thatcher warmed to the monetarist message. In Germany, the Bundesbank also started to pay specific attention to the speed at which money was being printed.

Problems with monetarism The problem is that, whether Friedman was right or wrong, it has proved so difficult to find an appropriate measure of money growth – the amount of money flowing around the economy – that putting his doctrine into practice has been too much of a challenge. Inflation may be a monetary phenomenon, but the amount of money in circulation often rises and falls for reasons that have nothing to do with inflation. When, for example, experts in the City or Wall Street devise a new type of financial instrument, it often pushes up the amount of money in the system. However, it is difficult or impossible to judge what is driving increases until well after the event, by which stage central bankers have already had to take their interest-rate decisions. This has meant that, in practice, attempts to control the amount of money in circulation have been abandoned by all but the European Central Bank, which retains one alongside its inflation target.

Volcker's successor at the Fed, Alan Greenspan, although an avowed free marketer with great respect for monetarism, was also responsible for ignoring the monetary statistics, to the extent that the Fed actually stopped publishing figures on money growth a few years ago.

Monetarism vs. Keynesianism – the outcome The result of the clash between Friedman and Keynes is, as is so often the case for contests between giants, a draw. Modern central banks tend to focus on both monetary and more traditional indicators when deciding on policy. Although the focus on money diminished in the late 1990s and early 2000s, it has returned more recently, with economists claiming the slump in money growth helped explain the economic downturn that followed the 2008 credit crisis.

On the other hand, there is a growing consensus that the kinds of policies suggested by Friedman, and espoused by Thatcher and Reagan in the 1980s – liberalizing financial markets, clamping down on inflation and money growth, giving companies more freedom to borrow and to hire and fire staff – were actually partly responsible for causing the build-up in debt that triggered the financial crisis. As economics commentator Martin Wolf said, shortly before the UK and US dipped into recession: 'Just as Keynes's ideas were tested to destruction in the 1950s, 1960s and 1970s, Milton Friedman's ideas might suffer a similar fate in the 1980s, 1990s and 2000s. All gods fail, if one believes too much.'

As for the two men themselves, they never met face to face. The only time they came into contact was in the 1930s when Friedman submitted a paper to the *Economic Journal*, a periodical that Keynes was editing at the time. The paper was a rather caustic attack on Keynes's fellow Cambridge economics professor A.C. Pigou. Keynes showed the paper to Pigou, who disagreed with the criticism, so Keynes wrote to Friedman telling him he'd decided not to publish it. 'That was one of only two letters I ever received from Keynes,' Friedman later remembered; 'the other also a rejection!'

the condensed idea
Control the growth of money

11 Communism

A few years ago the British Broadcasting Corporation asked its radio listeners to vote for their favourite philosopher. As the votes poured in there were some obvious favourites from the start – Plato, Socrates, Aristotle, Hume and Nietzsche among them – but as the counting started it soon transpired that there was a clear winner for the title of Britain's favourite philosopher: Karl Marx.

Not long afterwards, in late 2008, a German bookseller reported that sales of Marx's magnum opus *Das Kapital* were rocketing higher than they had for decades.

How was it that a radical German émigré whose ideas and predictions had been proven wrong again and again, and seemed to be laid to rest when the Berlin Wall fell, remains so popular? Why, in particular, should his works inspire so much devotion in a country that had not only rejected socialism but become one of the most free-market states in the world?

The famous theory Marx's key point was that societies are in the midst of a process of evolution from less sophisticated, less fair economic systems towards an ideal final destination. Having started off in feudal states and moved on through mercantilism to the modern system of capitalism, human society would naturally soon graduate to a fairer, more utopian system. That system, he argued, was communism.

In a communist society, property and the means of production (factories, tools, raw materials, etc.) would be owned not by private individuals or companies, but by everyone. Initially the state would own and control all

timeline

1848	1867	1883
The *Communist Manifesto* by Marx and Engels is published	The first volume of *Das Kapital* is published	Marx dies in London

KARL MARX 1818–83

Born to a middle-class Jewish/Protestant family, Marx spent most of his life either in university or writing his books. After university at Bonn and then Berlin, where he read law, history and philosophy and published a thesis on Greek philosopher Epicurus, he was drawn towards political theory. He became the editor of a newspaper with revolutionary leanings in 1842, suffering repeated censorship from the government. After the newspaper was closed down, he moved to Paris, where he met industrialist Friedrich Engels, with whom he later wrote *The Communist Manifesto* in 1848. Marx was banished from France and then Belgium, afterwards living until his death in London. He was largely supported throughout by the generosity of his friends – in particular Engels. When he died in 1883 the second and third volumes of his magnum opus *Das Kapital* had yet to be published; they were subsequently put together from his notes by Engels. He is buried in Highgate Cemetery in London.

companies and institutions, running them from the top down and ensuring companies did not oppress their workers. Eventually, however, the state would 'wither away'. This, said Marx, represented the final stage of human society, when the class barriers that had stratified nations for thousands of years would dissolve.

Class conflict Many forms of communism had been proposed before Marx and his colleague Friedrich Engels took it up in *The Communist Manifesto* in 1848. For example, in 1516 English writer and politician Thomas More sketched out a society based on common ownership of property in his book *Utopia*, and various communist communities had already cropped up in Europe and the United States by the early 19th century.

Marx's point, however, was that communism would be adopted en masse as workers throughout the world revolted against their governments and overthrew them to institute a fairer society. His rationale for this was that

1917
Russian Revolution puts Lenin in power, leading to the foundation of the Soviet Union

1949
Mao Zedong establishes the People's Republic of China as a communist state

1991
Under Mikhail Gorbachev, the Soviet Union dissolves itself

> **❝The theory of communism may be summed up in one sentence: Abolish all private property.❞**
>
> **Karl Marx**

the existing system of capitalism was patently unfair, the rich – with more capital (possessions) – becoming richer at the expense of the average worker. He claimed that human history was a history of class struggle, with conflict between the aristocracy and the rising bourgeoisie (the capitalist middle class, who increasingly owned the means of production) giving way to a new conflict between the bourgeoisie and the proletariat (the working classes who labour for them).

At the heart of Marx's theories was the labour theory of value. This idea, laid out in *Das Kapital* (1867), states that a commodity is worth the amount of time it takes for someone to make it. So, for instance, a jacket that takes twice as long as a pair of trousers to stitch and sew ought to be worth twice as much. However, he argued, those who ran companies pocketed disproportionate amounts of the profits themselves. The reason bosses get away with this, Marx argued, is that they own the means of production and so are able to exploit their workers. There are question marks over how well the labour theory of value holds up. However, the broad thrust remains undiminished: that there is a major divide between the wealth and opportunity of those who own land and capital and of those who do not.

Anyone reading the *Communist Manifesto* today might be surprised that the world it describes existed over a century and a half ago. It appears to be a very modern world, a world of globalization, downsizing, massive international corporations and so forth. Marx painted a picture in which competition between capitalists would become so ferocious that eventually most would either go bankrupt or find themselves taken over by others, leaving only a small band of monopolies controlling almost the entire production system, which in turn would have almost limitless power to exploit workers. He also predicted that since capitalism was inherently chaotic, it would be prone to ever-larger booms and busts over time, causing a series of major economic slumps and large rises in unemployment. This – coupled with the daily drudgery of doing the same repetitive job – would eventually become too much for the proletariat to bear, and revolution would ensue.

Communism in the modern world At one stage in the 20th century around half the world's population lived under governments that claimed Marx as their guiding political light. However, by the end of the century only a couple of unreconstructed dictatorships remained pure communist nations. Why did the theory not stand the test of time?

In part, because Marx was wrong about the eventual evolution of capitalism. It has not descended into a monopolistic system – at least not yet – thanks in part to government regulation and in part to the invisible hand (see chapter 1). The world did not become overrun with the unemployed, and, although booms and busts have continued (see chapter 31), government control is as much to blame for these as unbridled capitalist forces.

Few if any of the countries that embraced communism following socialist revolutions could strictly be said to fit Marx's criteria – they were mostly agrarian, low-income, undeveloped nations, such as Russia and China.

The 20th-century experiments with Marxism also underlined its inherent flaws. Most important of all, central control over an economy has proven immensely difficult to pull off – if not impossible. When the Iron Curtain fell in the 1990s and the former Soviet states were opened up to Western eyes, it became clear that, for all the bombast of the Cold War years, they were painfully underdeveloped.

While the forces of supply and demand created dynamic economies that generated wealth at a rapid rate, the staid, centrally controlled systems in the Soviet Union and China stifled innovation. Without competition between companies – the fundamental driving force of free markets – the economy simply trundled along, pushed forward by bureaucrats. There was only one area where the Soviets truly excelled: military and aeronautic innovation. Tellingly, this was the only field in which there was outright competition – in this case with the West in the Cold War.

the condensed idea
An egalitarian, entirely state-run society

12 Individualism

It was a phrase Karl Marx first used with disgust: 'The cult of the individual'. But by the late 20th century the idea that individual choices are of primary importance in economic policymaking had become dominant. This philosophy was the seed of Thatcherism and Reaganism, and it all stemmed from one small European nation: Austria.

Although economics is the study of why people take certain decisions, classical economics tended, for the sake of ease, to emphasize that people typically act in unison. For example, when a new type of potato chip hits the shelves and proves popular, it is because consumers are attracted to it. The Austrian School, however – which was born in the later 19th century and gained force in the 20th century – focused on the specific reasons each individual has for deciding to buy a particular product.

> **'There is no such thing as society: there are individual men and women, and there are families.'**
>
> **Margaret Thatcher**

Mainstream economics was – and still is – very much a top-down subject, examining the economic performance of a nation as a whole, or a sub-set of that country, by using aggregate measures (in other words, adding up the different parts to come to a grand total) such as gross domestic product and inflation. The Austrian School instead emphasizes that individual decision-making should be at the forefront. After all, only individuals can act; countries, companies and institutions do not have minds of their own – they are a collective entity, but one that comprises many different individuals.

Economic phenomena – a country's wealth or levels of inequality for instance – are a product of choices made by thousands of individuals,

timeline

1871
Principles of Economics by Carl Menger is published

1944
A key Austrian economics text, *The Road to Serfdom* by Friedrich Hayek, is published

rather than a consequence of the concerted policies of politicians or big business. The consequence is that there may not be any way of, for instance, reducing inequality to a certain level, since it is not the product of human design but a manifestation of human action.

Art or science? Fundamental to the Austrian theory of the primacy of the individual, is the idea that economics is more art than science. Such an idea may come as a surprise to those familiar with conventional academic economics, with its charts and equations. Using economic models, they would argue, it is possible to put a percentage chance on almost anything, from a change in interest rates or a period of recession to something apparently outside the economic field such as teenage pregnancy rates or even the likelihood of war.

However, despite the confidence of its practitioners, such scientific forecasts all too often get it wrong. As Bank of England Governor Mervyn King warns people when he presents his forecasts, the only thing he is 100 per cent sure about is that they will be proven wrong – there is no way of precisely predicting the future.

Although the father of the Austrian School, Carl Menger – whose *Principles of Economics* was published in 1871 – maintained that economics is still a social science, aiming to classify people's actions into a logical framework and set of patterns, his prime thrust was to stress the chaotic nature of economics. With this in mind, the Austrian economists avoid as far as possible inserting numbers and equations into their studies – a fact that has led to many of their papers being rejected by professional journals on the grounds that they contain insufficient facts, figures or equations.

> **‘A society that does not recognize that each individual has values of his own which he is entitled to follow can have no respect for the dignity of the individual and cannot really know freedom.’**
> **Friedrich Hayek, Austrian economist**

1955
The Institute of Economic Affairs – a think-tank that provided much of the intellectual backing for Thatcher – is founded

1974
Friedrich Hayek wins the Nobel Prize

A Martian in Grand Central Station

Imagine you're a Martian who has touched down on earth to find yourself in Grand Central Station in New York City. Every morning at around 8 a.m. you see the arrival of big rectangular boxes on wheels that spew people out into the concourse and off into the street. Then in the evening you see thousands of people herd themselves back into the boxes. By watching this behaviour each day you could devise some fairly reliable 'scientific' rules about human behaviour, and even predict precisely what people would do each day, without understanding why on earth they take part in this daily mass migration. You'd come up with a pretty blinkered view of humankind. This is precisely the criticism the Austrian School makes about orthodox economics, which devises complex models that take little account of individual human decision-making. The risk is that economists put so much faith in the models that they fail to see the ulterior motives behind people's decisions.

The generalization trap As Menger's successor, Nobel Prize-winning Austrian Friedrich Hayek, observed, everyone is different, and as such – although they might be treated in precisely the same way – the way they react to that treatment may differ greatly. The only way to ensure they are equal, he maintained, 'would be to treat them differently. Equality before the law and material equality are therefore not only different but are in conflict with each other; and we can achieve either one or the other, but not both at the same time.'

Take, for instance, a shopkeeper. Orthodox economics takes as one of its first assumptions the fact that he intends during the course of the day to maximize his profits – after all, this element of self-interest is one of the most important rules laid down by Adam Smith (see chapter 1). However, an Austrian economist would point out that the amount he sells could just as easily be determined by whether he decides to open up late, or whether he refuses to sell to a particular individual since he has a grudge against him. Personal factors such as these determine his behaviour, and, en masse, determine the behaviour of shopkeepers across the land.

Supply and demand, in the eyes of the Austrian economist, is an abstracted description of what causes prices to rise and fall – not itself a cause. Conventional economists counter that all social sciences need such abstractions and generalizations, but the chief achievement of Austrian economics is to force the science to consider that someone's values, plans, expectations, and understanding of reality are all subjective.

Individualism vindicated? But why is this so important? A school of thought that warns against making broad assumptions concerning human behaviour may seem less useful than orthodox economics, which attempts to forecast outcomes and provide solutions for policymakers through making just such assumptions. However, the scepticism of the Austrian School has been vindicated, not least because Hayek and his fellow-Austrian Ludwig von Mises were among the earliest to predict the demise of communism, arguing that a centrally planned state would fail since government planners would never have enough information about what drives their citizens to take individual decisions.

Austrian economists emphasize the importance of freeing up the individual to take his or her own choices. This laissez-faire ideal ultimately inspired some of the biggest reforms in 20th-century economics, for it was, at least in part, the ideas of the Austrian School that inspired both Ronald Reagan and Margaret Thatcher to push forward their free-market reforms, and that informed their supply-side reforms (see chapter 13). They recognized that the focus should not be on top-down economics, but on individuals' wants and desires.

> ‘Once it has been perceived that the division of labour is the essence of society, nothing remains of the antithesis between individual and society. The contradiction between individual principle and social principle disappears.’
>
> **Ludwig von Mises, Austrian economist**

the condensed idea
Individual human choices are paramount

13 Supply-side economics

The government raises taxes but rather than bringing in more money to its accounts this actually *reduces* its revenues. Conversely, cutting taxes brings in *more* cash. Economic logic has been turned on its head. But this is no black magic; it is instead the main tenet of supply-side economics.

Supply-side economics is among the most controversial of economic theories. The debate over it encapsulates the divide between those who believe in greater government distribution of wealth and those who believe, above all, in individual liberty and a free market.

> ❝When you cut the highest tax rates on the highest-income earners, government gets more money from them.❞
>
> **Arthur Laffer**

The term concerns more than just tax rates. Most broadly, supply-side economics refers to the reform of the supply side of the economy – meaning the institutions and companies that produce the goods people consume. In this traditional sense, supply-siders are those who would like these companies to be freer and more efficient; they support the privatization of utilities (such as water and energy companies), cuts in subsidies to struggling sectors (such as farming and mining), and the abolition of monopolies (such as telecommunications companies). There are, in fact, few economists who would argue with aims like these.

However, since the 1980s, 'supply-side economics' has tended to refer more specifically to arguments in favour of cutting high tax rates, an idea most

timeline

1940s	1970s
Governments worldwide raise taxes to unprecedented highs to pay off war debts and fund the creation of welfare systems	Arthur Laffer develops the idea of the Laffer Curve

notably propounded by American economist Arthur Laffer in the late 1970s. The more people have to pay in taxes, he argued, the greater will be people's incentive to avoid paying them or to work less hard.

The Laffer Curve Laffer argued that if a government levied no taxes it would (logically) receive no revenue; neither would any money pour into its coffers if it imposed 100 per cent taxes (because no one would have any incentive to work). He then sketched out (on the back of a napkin, so legend has it) a bell-shaped curve which showed that there was a point somewhere between zero and 100 per cent where a government could get maximum potential revenues. The argument – that lower taxes could actually increase government revenues – found admirers in Ronald Reagan and Margaret Thatcher.

Flat taxes

The apotheosis of supply-side economics is the flat tax, in which everyone pays the same rate. It is a system that has been taken up with particular vigour by some of the former communist republics, including Latvia and Estonia. They have found that more people now pay their taxes, which has pushed up tax revenues – despite the cut in the headline rate of tax.

The theory focuses particularly on the *marginal tax rate* – the rate one pays on every extra hour of work one does. Many of the biggest economies, including the US and the UK, had marginal rates of around 70 per cent. Since workers will take home only 30 per cent of every extra pound or dollar they earn, this clearly affects the incentive people have to work longer hours.

A vivid example of this occurred when, in 2008, the UK Treasury pledged, for the first time since the 1970s, to raise the top level of tax. It ordained that the tax rate for any income above £150,000 would be 45 per cent, compared with the previous top tax rate of just 40 per cent. However, leading tax experts calculated that this would bring in no extra revenues whatsoever, since it would deter people from working longer hours. Indeed, they warned, such a measure could just as easily reduce tax revenues.

early 1980s	**late 1980s**	**1994**	**1995**
Laffer's ideas are embraced by Thatcher and Reagan	Taxes are cut in the UK, US and across the Western world	Estonia introduces flat taxes	Latvia follows suit

Positively negative

Another radical idea came from Milton Friedman (see chapter 10). He argued for the creation of a negative income tax. The point is that the state already has to redistribute cash to poorer families in the form of social security and unemployment benefits. If, instead, there was a negative income tax system, those who earn above a certain amount would pay their taxes as normal, while those who earned less would actually receive negative taxes – in other words an instant rebate – from the taxman. The idea is that it could eliminate the cumbersome and expensive social security and unemployment benefit infrastructure.

The problem is not only that people will find ways to avoid paying extra tax by, for example, decamping to tax havens such as Monaco or the Cayman Islands, but also that higher marginal tax rates can damage the overall economy. Discouraging the workers who generate the most money (usually those on higher wages) will drive them out of the country or away from their jobs, reducing an economy's overall wealth creation. If this happens, it is a sign that the country's government should either consider cutting taxes or find other incentives for encouraging businesses to stay.

By contrast, when tax rates are low, it encourages people to work longer hours, although the respective share the government takes of every extra dollar earned is less. The Laffer Curve illustrates that the government must strike a balance between the two, expressing scientifically the truth of the dictum of Louis XIV's finance minister, Jean-Baptiste Colbert, that taxation is the art of 'so plucking the goose as to get the most feathers with the least hissing'.

How high is too high? The big question – given the Laffer Curve's indication that beyond a certain point tax rates bring in less and less revenue – is where that cut-off point lies. Certainly not at the 90 per cent marginal rates paid by some in the 1960s, nor at a rate of 15 per cent, which could leave the government unable to finance its welfare state and social spending.

The debate continues to rage today, with many left-leaning economists proposing that the ceiling should be over 50 per cent, while those at the other end of the political spectrum suggest it should be below 40.

Throughout the world the consensus has been towards lower marginal rates. The number of countries with a top tax rate of 60 per cent or above had dropped from 49 in 1980 to just 3 by the turn of the millennium – Belgium, Cameroon and the Democratic Republic of Congo.

> ‘The more government takes in taxes,
> the less incentive people have to work.
> What coal miner or assembly-line worker
> jumps at the offer of overtime when
> he knows Uncle Sam is going to take
> 60 percent or more of his extra pay?’
>
> **Ronald Reagan**

Laffer problems While it is difficult to dispute the elegant logic of the Laffer hypothesis, there remain major questions as to whether it actually works in practice. Indeed, in the early 1980s Reagan's tax cuts were derided by George H.W. Bush as 'voodoo economics'. According to Harvard professor Jeffrey Frankel the theory, 'while theoretically possible under certain conditions, does not apply to US income tax rates: a cut in those rates reduces revenue, precisely as common sense would indicate'.

Indeed, evidence shows that the Reagan tax cuts and the George W. Bush cuts in 2001–3 reduced government revenues and pushed the budget deficit higher. In other words, they were unfunded, and would have to be paid back eventually. Supply-siders maintain that what the administration got wrong was the choice of particular taxes to cut, rather than the decision to reduce the overall level of taxation.

Although the hypothesis remains extremely popular to this day (perhaps because it promises politicians something for nothing), study after study has disproved its effectiveness. Only in extreme cases – with rates being massively high, for instance – can cuts in taxes bring in higher revenues.

That said, there is little doubt that excessively high taxes can hold back economic growth. By highlighting this argument, supply-side economics has been responsible for a wholesale overhaul in the way taxes are perceived and constructed throughout the world.

the condensed idea
Higher taxes mean lower growth

14 The marginal revolution

In 2007 David Beckham made waves around the world by signing a five-year deal to move from Real Madrid in Spain to Major League soccer club LA Galaxy for a reported $250 million. It was the size of the deal that generated most interest. He may have been a good soccer star; he may also have been a massive marketing draw for both the soccer club and the league, which has struggled to compete with NFL, NBA and other American sports. But, really . . . $250 million for one man?

Uneconomic though it may sound, the price paid seems in fact to have been a good one. The soccer club would not have paid it had it not expected to generate a healthy profit from the deal. Indirectly then, it is the public who consider Beckham, and footballers like him, worth that kind of price. They are willing to pay for Beckham-related products – everything from soccer shirts with his name on them to the clothes and razors he promotes.

The margin Why is it that we place so much more value on one human being than another? Great athletes may be good at their sport, but why do they earn far more than even those whose roles are essential for our well-being – teachers or doctors for example? The answer is to be found at what economists call *the margin*.

Some three hundred years ago, Adam Smith mentioned a not dissimilar paradox to the Beckham one in *The Wealth of Nations*. Why, he asked, was

timeline

1700	**1776**
Early mercantilists start to recognize ideas of marginal utility	Adam Smith cites the water/diamonds paradox in *The Wealth of Nations*

there such a difference in price between diamonds and water? Unlike water, diamonds are not essential for human existence; they are pieces of crystalline carbon – albeit highly attractive ones. He reasoned that more work goes into making a diamond – mining it, cutting it, polishing it and so on – than providing water, which thus justifies the cost. Diamonds, moreover, are scarce, whereas water is plentiful for most of us in the Western world.

> **It is on the margin, and not with a view to the big picture, that we make economic decisions.**
>
> **Eugen von Böhm-Bawerk, Austrian economist**

In the same way, there are only a small number of people who have David Beckham's ability to swerve a ball round a wall and score from free kicks. Scarcity pushes up the price. However, this is only half of the explanation. After all, there is just as scarce a supply of highly talented fencers in the world, and yet they are unlikely to earn even Beckham's weekly wage over many years.

The answer to the paradox, which was proposed by economists in the late 19th century (including Carl Menger of the Austrian School; see chapter 12), is that the value of a given thing – whether it is David Beckham, a diamond or a glass of water – is subjective. It depends entirely on how people value that thing at a given moment. The point sounds simple but it turned out to be revolutionary. Previously, people assumed something had an inherent value; after the marginal revolution it became clear that things have value only insofar as people want them.

Marginal utility Let's go back to our glass of water. To someone who has endured days of thirst in a desert, that glass is invaluable; they would probably pay any amount of cash for it, even a diamond, if they had it. But the more glasses that are available to that person, the less they will be willing to pay. We need to determine the value not of all the water in the world but of each particular glass. And the satisfaction one would get from

1871

Carl Menger proposes marginalism

1890

Alfred Marshall popularizes marginal utility in his *Principles of Economics*

each extra serving of water is what economists would call the *marginal utility* of each glass. In this case, there is a diminishing marginal utility.

There are numerous examples of prices that have increased or decreased because the marginal utility of the commodity in question rose or fell. Oil prices were down at around only $20 a barrel in the early years of the 21st century, but only a few years later they vaulted up above $100 a barrel, at one point touching $140. Fears over supply, exacerbated by demand from fast-growing economies, meant that people were willing to pay higher prices. Then, only months later, the price plummeted back to below $40 a barrel again as the world economy suffered recession.

The idea of marginal utility blossomed under another of the great economists, Alfred Marshall (1842–1924), who propounded the idea that consumers take decisions based on marginal considerations. Previously, attention had focused more on supply than demand, but he argued that this one-sided approach was comparable to trying to cut a piece of paper

All you can eat

Most of us have at one point or other been tempted into a restaurant by the offer of an all-you-can-eat flat-fee buffet. You pay the money up front – let's say $10.99 – and start eating. In economics terms, the overall cost remains the same – $10.99 – but the marginal cost, in other words for each extra portion, is zero because that's how much extra it costs you. However, the actual amount of enjoyment and satisfaction provided by the food (what economists call 'utility') diminishes with each portion as we get fuller and fuller and perhaps even sicker and sicker.

So while the marginal cost of one extra portion is zero, the marginal utility starts high and falls. The same principle is universal in economics. We tend to derive more pleasure from our first consumption of a particular good, but thereafter the returns diminish – just as a stamp collector's first acquisition of a Penny Black is more satisfying than his second, third or fourth.

(the paper being the price) with just one blade of a pair of scissors. Instead of considering something – say, a glass of water – to have a particular price, determined by the costs to the supplier of sourcing it and bottling it, Marshall emphasized that consumers' desires should also be considered. They will only buy a product, he argued, if the item: (1) looks attractive to them; (2) is affordable; and (3) is reasonably priced in comparison to other goods. Each of these considerations affects the marginal price, whether it be for a glass of water or a world-famous soccer player.

Thinking at the margin Marshall's emphasis was on the marginal; people only do something – be it manufacturing light bulbs or cramming for an exam the following day – as long as that extra work or light bulb is worthwhile. At a certain stage sleeping will become a more sensible plan than working through the early hours; likewise the revenue from producing a new bulb will become less than the cost of production. We all think at the margin – it is the practical way to behave. Economies, therefore, advance in incremental steps rather than in giant leaps. The marginal revolution was what shed light on the true nature of economic evolution.

While all humans are by nature marginalists, it took Marshall to establish the idea of marginal utility as part of the economics bedrock. Now, such ideas inform business plans across the world. They are central to commerce.

Neither does the Beckham parable end there. Two years after the footballer's move, he was involved in a tug-of-war with Italian club AC Milan. The spat again underlined the importance of marginal utility considerations. The Italians considered a flat face-value fee would be enough for the player. But Tim Leiweke, chief executive of LA Galaxy, said: 'What Milan don't understand is that behind this story there are fans that are renouncing their subscriptions and sponsors that want damages.' This is a classic example of marginal thinking.

the condensed idea
Rational people think at the margin

15 Money

Economics isn't all about money, but money makes economists of us all. Ask someone to pay a price for something – as opposed to offering it for free, or for a favour – and you'll flick an invisible switch inside them.

Behavioural economist Dan Ariely used an experiment to prove this. He offered students a piece of Starbucks candy at a cost of 1 cent each. On average they took four pieces. Then he changed the price to zero – free. Traditional economics would assume that, with the price lower, demand would increase (see chapter 2), but no. Once money had been taken out of the equation, something strange happened. Almost none of the students took more than one piece each.

Money makes the world go round Money is one of the key elements in an economy. Without it, we would be forced to barter, i.e. exchange goods or offer someone a favour or a service in order to pay for something. Just as communication becomes far easier when both participants in a conversation have a common language, as opposed to relying on gestures and noises, so money provides a simple medium of exchange without which every transaction simply becomes unbearably complicated.

In countries where people lose faith in money – perhaps because of hyperinflation – they often resort to a barter economy. When the Soviet Union was collapsing in the late 1980s many started to use cigarettes as currency. However, barter economies are highly inefficient – imagine having to come up with a different compelling offer of services or goods every time you wanted to visit the shops. You might as well stay at home.

> **❝Money is the sinew of love as well as war.❞**
> **Thomas Fuller**

timeline

c10000 BC	3000 BC	600 BC
First evidence of bartering in parts of Africa	Shekels (units of weight) traded in Mesopotamia	First evidence of gold and silver coins in Lydia

In addition to this primary function as a medium of exchange, money has two other purposes. First, it is a unit of account, meaning it is a yardstick against which things can be priced, helping us to judge the value of something. Second, it is a store of value, meaning it will not lose its worth over time – though it is debatable whether modern paper currencies fulfil this function. We are all familiar with what constitutes money – whether it be dollar bills, pound coins, euro cents or other types of currency – but technically any kind of tradable unit can be treated as money: for example, shells, jewellery, cigarettes and drugs (the last two often serve as money in prisons). And, more than ever before, money today constitutes invisible flows of credit – borrowed money – between lenders and borrowers.

Liquidity

Liquidity is a measure of how easy it is for someone to exchange an asset – for instance a house, a gold bar or a pack of cigarettes – for money or other types of currency. For instance, the shares in most big companies are usually highly liquid – they can be easily sold because there are usually plenty of buyers. Houses are more illiquid since it takes time to organize a property sale. When businesses have liquidation sales, it simply means they are attempting to sell off all their goods for cash.

Types of money It is possible to distinguish between two major categories of money:

Commodity money This has intrinsic value, even though it is not actually a form of money. Gold is perhaps the most obvious example, since it can be used to make jewellery and is a key metal for use in industry. Other types of commodity money include silver, copper, foods (like rice and peppercorns), alcohol, cigarettes and drugs.

Fiat money This is money without intrinsic value. From the Latin 'let it be', it simply means that a government has decreed that coins and notes of negligible intrinsic value are legally worth a certain amount. This is the

AD**800s**

China invents first banknotes

1816

Introduction of the gold standard, pegging all money to a set amount of gold

The history of money

For hundreds of thousands of years human civilizations tended to barter for goods, trading shells and precious stones for food and other important commodities. For the first evidence of money as a currency, we need to go back 5,000 years to where modern-day Iraq now sits, to find the shekel. Though this was the first form of currency, it wasn't money as we know and understand it. It actually represented a certain weight of barley equivalent to gold or silver. Eventually the shekel became a coin currency in its own right. In much the same way, Britain's currency is called the pound because it was originally equivalent to a pound of silver.

The ancient Greeks and Romans used gold and silver coins as currency, with the Latin denarius ultimately giving birth to the dinar in various countries, including Jordan and Algeria, and providing the 'd' that served as an abbreviation for the British penny before decimalization in 1971. It also gives us the word for money in Spanish and Portuguese – *dinero* and *dinheiro*.

The first ever banknotes were issued in 7th-century China, though it took another 1,000 years before the idea of paper money was adopted in Europe, by Sweden's Stockholms Banco in 1661.

system in place in modern advanced economies. Dollar bills are issued by the Federal Reserve and the US Treasury, and £5, £10 and £20 notes (and so on) are issued by the Bank of England. Originally, paper money was convertible into commodity money, so that, technically, citizens could demand a certain amount of gold in exchange for their dollar bills. However, since 15 August 1971, following an order from President Nixon, convertibility stopped and the dollar became a pure fiat currency. Fiat currencies are reliant for their stability on people's faith in the country's legal system and in the government's economic credibility.

> **'So you think that money is the root of all evil. Have you ever asked what is the root of all money?'**
>
> Ayn Rand

Measuring money Measuring how much money is flowing round an economy is one of the key ways to determine that economy's health. When people have more money, they feel wealthier and tend to spend more, while businesses respond to their increased sales by ordering more raw materials and raising production. This in turn pushes up share prices and economic growth.

Central banks measure money in various ways. The most popular is what the Federal Reserve calls M1. This measures the amount of currency in circulation outside banks and the amount of funds people have left in their bank accounts. In other words, M1 represents how much cash people have readily available. There are also other, broader measures of money: M2, which includes less liquid (readily accessible) assets such as savings accounts that require notice for withdrawals; and M3, which covers financial instruments regarded by many as close substitutes for money, such as long-term savings and money-market funds. For some reason, in the UK the Bank of England's equivalent of M3 is called M4.

At the turn of the millennium, there was around $580 billion worth of US dollars floating around, while there was a further $599 billion sitting in people's instant-access bank accounts. If you divide the amount of currency by every US adult – 212 million – this implies that each adult holds around $2,736 of currency, which is clearly more than most people hold in their wallets. The reason the apparent per capita share is so high is partly because much of the money is actually held overseas, since dollars are used as currency in many countries other than the US, and partly because some people – for example criminals, including those who work in the black market – prefer to keep their money in cash rather than putting it in a bank account.

> **Money never made a man happy yet, nor will it. The more a man has, the more he wants. Instead of filling a vacuum, it makes one.**
> **Benjamin Franklin**

Money is more than merely currency. It is more, even, than the stock of currency in circulation and in people's bank accounts. It is also a state of mind. The paper notes and brass and nickel coins we carry around in our pockets are worth only a fraction of the amount they denominate – and the electronic transfer of cash from one bank account to another has even less intrinsic value. Which is why money must be backed up by trust – trust both that the payer is good for his cash and that the government will ensure the money is worth something in the future.

the condensed idea
Money is a token of trust

16 Micro and macro

Economics actually comprises two subjects. First, it's the technical specialism of studying how and why people take certain decisions. Second, it's the broad study of how governments improve growth, tackle inflation, maintain their finances and ensure unemployment does not climb too high. The distinction between microeconomics and macroeconomics is central to understanding economics.

'Micro or macro?' is usually the first question newly introduced economists ask each other, the distinction between the two approaches running to the heart of economics. They are usually regarded by hard-and-fast economists as completely separate fields of study, to the point that many spend their entire life specializing in one or the other, without any sense of missing out.

What's the difference? Deriving from *mikros*, ancient Greek for 'small', microeconomics is the term used for the study of how households and businesses make their decisions and interact with markets. For instance, a micro specialist might focus on how a particular type of arable farming has risen and fallen in recent years.

The term macroeconomics comes from the Greek *makros* – 'large' – and is the study of how economies as a whole function. A macroeconomist is more interested in questions about why a country's growth rate is so strong

timeline

1930	1933
Great Depression causes a split between individual human behaviour and aggregate behaviour	First use of the term macroeconomics, by Norwegian economist Ragnar Frisch

> **⁶Microeconomics: The study of who has the money and how I can get my hands on it. Macroeconomics: The study of which government agency has the gun, and how we can get our hands on it.⁹**
>
> **Gary North, US journalist**

but inflation low (as with the United States throughout most of the 1990s), or what are the causes of rising inequality (as witnessed for example in both the UK and US over recent decades).

Roots of the distinction Why the split? A good question – indeed, until the mid-20th century no such divide existed. An economist was just an economist. Those who focused on the larger scale called themselves monetary economists, while those who studied the small were called price theorists. In fact, economists tended to think far more on the small scale. Then along came John Maynard Keynes, who transformed perceptions of the subject (see chapter 9). In essence, he created macroeconomics, with all its emphasis on the role of states, both at home (in terms of using public money and interest rates to try to keep the economy on track) and internationally (in terms of monitoring trade with other nations).

Microeconomics, on the other hand, has grown to become a massive area of study of its own accord. It is most particularly focused on the way in which supply and demand interact in various circumstances (see chapter 2). It examines people's reaction to taxes and regulations, to changes in prices or tastes, but stops short of drawing conclusions about the effect this will have on an entire economy. That is the job of the macroeconomist. The two are interrelated, of course, but what makes them different subjects is that micro focuses on one market in isolation whereas macro looks at all markets collectively.

1950s
Macroeconomics gains popularity along with Keynesianism

1990s
Microeconomics proliferates during a period of relative macroeconomic calm

This necessarily means that macroeconomists often have to make very broad assumptions about the behaviour of an economy, including the assumption that it will tend in the long run towards equilibrium between supply and demand – an assumption that is very much under debate.

A difference of approach Reports about economics in the quality press usually focus on macroeconomics: a change in interest rates or inflation across an economy; the overall output or Gross Domestic Product of a country; news of a recession or a major economic boom; the finance minister's economic message in his latest budget; and so forth. Usually you can tell a macro story since it has a top-down approach.

However, stories that focus on personal finance – about the effect taxes and other government measures are likely to have on people's day-to-day

Positive and normative economics

Positive economics is the empirical study of what is happening in the world. It examines, for example, why some countries are getting richer, why certain families are getting poorer, and what is likely to happen to them in the future. It avoids making any value judgements about whether certain phenomena ought to occur, being concerned simply with the scientific study of why they do.

Normative economics, on the other hand, engages with what is happening in the world and attempts to sketch out how the economy could be improved. As such it involves making value judgements about particular phenomena.

Take, for example, the following statement: 'A billion of the world's population live on less than $1 a day. This sum is below what any human should be expected to live on, and ought to be increased through aid and assistance from governments – particularly rich ones.' The first sentence is a positive economic statement; the latter is normative.

lives – are more firmly grounded in micro. They look at matters from the bottom up.

For instance, Gordon Brown, when he was the British Chancellor of the Exchequer, was frequently berated for attempting to micro-manage the economy. What this meant was that he eschewed big changes in income tax and interest rates, preferring to rely instead on smaller measures such as tax credits focused very specifically on particular types of families or on encouraging businesses to invest.

While there are relatively few schools of macroeconomics, micro specialists are lucky enough to have numerous fields of study upon which to focus. In what is called *applied economics* one can find a great range of specialists: those who look at employment and changes in the job market over time; public finance experts whose job it is to examine a government's accounts; experts on tax in relation to commodities or types of income or business taxes; agricultural and tariff specialists; wage experts; and so on.

Microeconomics is also much more heavily based on statistics than macro, with its practitioners often creating complex computer models to demonstrate how supply and demand will react to a particular change: how, for instance, the cost for car manufacturers will increase if oil prices (and hence energy costs) suddenly leap. A macroeconomist is much more concerned with the effect a rise in the oil price will have on an economy's overall growth rate, and with diagnosing why oil prices have spiked in the first place and how they can be brought back under control.

Nevertheless, although the two subjects are often treated separately, they are underpinned by the same fundamental rules: the interplay of supply and demand, the importance of prices and of properly functioning markets, and the need to determine how people act when faced with scarcity and a whole gamut of incentives.

the condensed idea
Micro for businesses, macro for countries

17 Gross domestic product

If there is one figure worth knowing in economics then it is surely that of gross domestic product (GDP). It is literally the biggest economic statistic of them all, dwarfing everything else, from inflation and unemployment to exchange rates and house prices.

A country's GDP is quite simply the measure of its entire income (gross = entire; domestic = in a particular economy; product = economic output, or activity). It is the most widely recognized measure of a country's economic strength and performance.

Most people are well aware that China has had a remarkable rise towards economic pre-eminence in recent decades. The GDP statistics (see opposite page) show that it has quickly leapfrogged France, Britain and Germany in recent years, and if it maintains its current rate of growth by 2010 it will have overtaken Japan as the world's second-largest economy. However, its economic output still remains a fraction of the size of that of the United States.

What does GDP include? Gross domestic product measures two things: the total income of the country and its total spending. Across an economy, income and expenditure equal each other. If you pay a dollar for a newspaper, that money – your expenditure – instantly becomes someone else's earnings. GDP measures both goods (such as food) and services (such as haircuts), including invisible items (such as housing services – the amount people pay to live in their homes, whether they rent or buy).

timeline

1950s

World embarks on a golden post-war period of economic growth

What is not included? The main exclusion is anything produced by the so-called informal economy. This includes trade in illegal goods (such as drugs and anything on the black market) which is thought to account for almost one-tenth of the economy in most rich countries. GDP also does not include the constituents of products as well as the products themselves. For instance, a car engine would not be counted separately from the finished vehicle of which it is a part. If the engine is sold off separately that is another matter.

What about foreign-owned companies?

GDP measures the value of anything produced within a certain country, whoever owns it. Thus, if a US company owns a factory in Mexico, that factory's output contributes to Mexico's GDP. However, there is another related statistic that measures the economic output of a country's citizens, whether they are based at home or abroad. The US's gross national product (GNP), for example, includes income earned by US citizens at home and abroad, but excludes what citizens and companies from other countries earn in the US. The figures for GDP and GNP are usually very similar.

How is GDP measured? When governments publish their GDP figures, they usually do so at quarterly intervals (i.e. every three months) and the figure that is of most interest is not the total amount but the growth rate. It is worth bearing in mind that the GDP growth rates most frequently quoted in newspapers or by politicians are for *real* GDP growth – in other words, they have had the effects of inflation stripped out. When the changes in market prices due to inflation are left in, the resulting figure is called *nominal GDP*.

GDP by country

	($ billion, 2008)
• United States	14,334
• Japan	4,844
• China	4,222
• Germany	3,818
• France	2,987
• United Kingdom	2,878
• Italy	2,399
• **World**	60,109
• **European Union**	19,195

Source: International Monetary Fund

1972
Bhutan starts to develop a gross national happiness index

2007
Longest stretch of global economic growth in decades draws to a close

What does GDP comprise? Rather like a tangerine, GDP is made up of various segments, each of which represents an important contribution to a country's economic growth. What a country spends money on can be accounted for as follows:

consumption + investment + government spending + net exports

Consumption means all the money that households spend on goods and services, and in rich countries it has, in recent decades, been by far the largest segment. In 2005 it accounted for 70 per cent of all spending in the US and much the same in the UK.

Investment is the cash poured into business on a relatively long-term basis, for instance to build new factories or buildings. It also includes the money families spend on buying newly built homes. It accounts for 16.9 per cent of US GDP and 16.7 per cent of UK GDP.

Government spending includes what national and local government bodies spend on goods and services. It accounts for 18.9 per cent of US GDP, but is far higher in most European countries, which have government-funded health services. In Britain it sat at around the 40 per cent level for most of the 1990s and 2000s. But there and in almost all rich countries the proportion increased sharply in the wake of the 2008 financial and economic crisis, as governments sought Keynesian solutions for their recessions (see chapter 9), pumping extra public cash into the economy.

You might have noticed that if you add these constituents up, they show that Americans are effectively spending more than 100 per cent of their GDP – 5.8 per cent more to be precise. How is this possible? In short, it is because in recent years the US has made up for the shortfall in domestically produced goods by importing from overseas. In 2005, exports accounted for 10.4 per cent of GDP while imports made up 16.2 per cent, the difference between the two – in other words the *net exports* – corresponding to that 5.8 per cent shortfall. This so-called trade deficit has sparked warnings that the US has been living beyond its means (see chapter 24).

Measuring economic performance using GDP Given that GDP is the broadest measure of an economy's performance, it is absolutely central to economics. Politicians are often judged on it, and economists try their hardest to predict what it will be. When the economy contracts it typically goes hand in hand with a rise in unemployment and falling wages. If it shrinks for two successive quarters, then the economy is technically in recession. Although this is a widely accepted definition for recession, in the US the 'R' word is not officially applied until the economic situation has been so judged by the National Bureau of Economic Research. The worst recessions of all are generally called depressions. There is no broadly accepted definition for a depression, although many economists stipulate that an economy must shrink by some 10 per cent from peak to trough. They generally agree that a depression constitutes well over a year of shrinking output. During the Great Depression in the 1930s America's GDP shrank by one-third.

Nevertheless, this versatile economic statistic has some important limitations. What, for instance, if a country suddenly opened its doors to many more immigrants or demanded that its citizens worked longer hours? This could push up GDP dramatically, even though the country's workers have not individually become any more productive. Thus, when gauging the health of an economy, statisticians prefer to look at its productivity – calculated by dividing GDP by the number of hours a country's citizens have worked. Another way to view GDP is by dividing it by the total population, so producing the figure for GDP per capita, which is often used by economists as an illustration of a country's standard of living.

> ❝It can be said without exaggeration that in the long run probably nothing is as important for economic welfare as the rate of productivity growth.❞
>
> **William J. Baumol, Sue Anne Blackman and Edward N. Wolff**

Although GDP is often held to reflect a nation's well-being, modern economists are aware of its limitations in this respect. For instance, GDP takes no account of potential inequality between different members of society. Neither does it pretend to measure environmental or social quality, nor individuals' happiness. For those one has to look elsewhere (see chapter 49). However, no statistic can compete with GDP in showing instantly whether a country's economy is thriving or stagnating.

the condensed idea
The key yardstick of a country's economic performance

18 Central banks and interest rates

The job of a central banker, said William McChesney Martin, is to 'take away the punch bowl just when the party gets going'. The legendary former Chairman of the Federal Reserve meant that it is up to the man or woman in charge of a country's monetary policy – its interest rates – to ensure that the economy neither overheats nor sinks into depression.

When the economy is roaring ahead and businesses are making record profits, there is a danger of inflation getting out of hand, and it is the central bank's unenviable task to try to bring the party to a civilized end, usually by raising interest rates. And if all goes wrong and the economy slumps, it is their job to prevent it suffering too nasty a hangover by cutting interest rates again. If that already sounds difficult, bear in mind that not even the central bank can know precisely how fast the economy is expanding at any given moment.

How central banks work The problem is that most of the statistics upon which central banks base their decisions are, by definition, out of date by the time they are published. Inflation figures – which are among the most promptly produced around the world – refer to the previous month. More fundamentally, because it takes time for the actual effects of certain changes in the economy to manifest themselves statistically (for instance, it takes weeks or even months for higher oil or metal prices to push up consumer prices), central banks have to drive the economy while looking out of the rear-view mirror rather than the front window.

timeline

1668
The Riksbank, the world's first central bank, is founded in Sweden

1694
The Bank of England is founded

The big four

• **The Federal Reserve (US)** Its chief decision-making body is the Federal Open Market Committee. Chaired by the Fed Chairman (Ben Bernanke, at the time of writing), this 12-member group, with representatives from regional reserve banks and federal appointees, decides interest rates in the world's biggest economy. Its previous chairman, Alan Greenspan, was so revered that, towards the end of his nearly 20-year term, he was nicknamed 'Oracle' and 'Maestro'.

• **The European Central Bank (Europe)** Its rates are decided by the governing council of 21 members, though in effect the ECB's president (currently Jean-Claude Trichet) takes the final decision.

• **Bank of Japan** This sets interest rates in the world's second-largest economy. Although it has been independent since the Second World War, some economists suspect it is more swayed by political forces than other central banks.

• **Bank of England** Although this is the second-oldest central bank, it was among the last to become independent of politicians, following Chancellor Gordon Brown's decision in 1997 to free it from government control. Rates are decided by the Monetary Policy Committee (MPC) of nine men and women. The Bank is nicknamed the 'Old Lady of Threadneedle Street', referring to the street in the City of London where it is situated.

Almost every country with its own currency and a government able to impose taxes has a central bank, ranging from the Fed (as most people call the US central bank) and the Bank of England (which actually determines interest rates for all of the United Kingdom) to the highly respected Swiss National Bank and the innovative Reserve Bank of New Zealand. The European Central Bank sets interest rates for all countries in the European Union that use the euro.

Most central banks operate independently of politics, though their leading executives are usually appointed – or at the very least vetted – by politicians. To ensure there is a check on these unelected individuals, they are usually given a remit, which can be specific, as in the case of the UK

1913
The US Federal Reserve set up by Woodrow Wilson

1998
The European Central Bank established in preparation for the launch of the euro

and euro area (a Consumer Price Index inflation target of 2 per cent) or more vague, as in the US (to entrench growth and prosperity).

How interest rates shape the economy Targets have changed over time. When, for instance, monetarism was in vogue in the 1980s, some central banks attempted to keep the growth in the money supply at a particular level. Nowadays, most central banks are more concerned with keeping inflation under control. Either way, the primary tool at a central bank's disposal for influencing the economy is its interest rate.

Lower interest rates generally mean a faster-growing economy and potentially higher inflation as a consequence, since saving is less lucrative, and borrowing and spending are more attractive options. The situation is reversed with higher rates.

In general, most central banks set a base rate (this is called the Fed Funds Rate in the US and the Bank Rate in the UK) on which other private banks base their own interest rates. In order to set this rate, policymakers in central banks have various levers to pull. First, they announce that they are changing their rate, and private banks usually follow suit and change their own mortgage, lending and savings rates accordingly. Second, they use open-market operations, which means buying and selling government bonds in order to influence the interest rates throughout the bond markets (see chapter 27). Third, they capitalize on the fact that all commercial banks are obliged to store a slice of their own funds in the central bank's vaults (these are known as reserves). Central banks can change the rate of interest they pay out on these reserves, or can order banks to hold more or less reserves, influencing how much they want to lend out to their customers, which in turn influences the interest rate.

The vast majority of these levers are invisible to consumers; what matters is the instant chain reaction they trigger, causing banks around the country to change the level of borrowing costs. The specifics of the levers only really matter when one or a number of them is broken, as can happen when money markets malfunction (see chapter 33).

Although the banks tend to make an interest-rate decision every month or couple of months, they have hundreds of employees permanently at work monitoring actual rates of borrowing in the market to ensure that the medicine they prescribe is actually working. During the financial crisis of the late 2000s central banks around the world had to devise a number of novel ways to pump extra money into the economy.

Inflation isn't the only thing affected by interest rates, however. Higher interest rates often strengthen a country's currency as investors from around the world channel their funds into buying it. The downside of this is that a stronger currency makes a country's exports more expensive for overseas customers.

Supporting the financial system The role of central banks is not just to control interest rates but also, more broadly, to ensure that the underlying financial system of an economy is in good health. As such, they also act as a lender of last resort in times of economic turbulence. When all is well in Wall Street and the City, for example, such a role is rarely necessary, since banks can generally borrow more cheaply and easily from their peers. At other times, however, the central bank's emergency lending becomes an essential life-jacket.

One of the many repercussions of the 2008 financial crisis has been to force central banks to enhance their lender-of-last-resort role in order to rescue stricken banks. In a break with decades of convention, for instance, the Fed started lending cash directly to hedge funds because everyone – bar the government – was finding it almost impossible to borrow money. They also started to buy up assets and pump extra cash into the economy through a process called quantitative easing (see chapter 20).

However, as always in economics, there is no such thing as a free lunch – for consumers or for banks. This greater generosity has come at the cost of more stringent regulation in the future. Interest rates will continue to be a major policy tool for central banks, but their power to monitor and regulate the financial system is also very much in the ascendancy.

> **'In central banking as in diplomacy, style, conservative tailoring, and an easy association with the affluent, count greatly and results far much less.'**
>
> **John Kenneth Galbraith**

the condensed idea
Central banks steer economies away from booms and busts

19 Inflation

Depending on whom you listen to, inflation will either clean your teeth or knock them out. Former United States President Ronald Reagan described it as being 'as violent as a mugger, as frightening as an armed robber and as deadly as a hit man'. Karl Otto Pöhl, former president of the German Bundesbank, said: 'Inflation is like toothpaste; once it's out [of the tube], you can hardly get it back in again.'

In fact, most of the time, inflation – the phenomenon of rising prices – is neither of the above. Keeping prices ticking up slowly and predictably has become one of the most important roles – if not *the* most important role – of central banks and governments when managing their economies. But inflation can have a nasty tendency to get out of control.

Levels of inflation Inflation is usually expressed on an annual basis. Thus, a 3 per cent inflation rate means that prices across the economy as a whole are 3 per cent higher than 12 months earlier.

Among the most telling of all economic statistics, inflation can help illustrate whether an economy is in good health, overheating or slowing down sharply. Too high and an economy risks becoming trapped in an inflationary spiral – when prices rise exponentially – or even hyperinflation; the difference between the two depends on the magnitude of price rises. Hyperinflation, which afflicted Germany in the 1920s and Zimbabwe during the first decade of the new millennium, involves price rises of at least 50 per cent – and often far higher – in a single month. Weimar Germany at one point had to resort to issuing banknotes of 100 trillion marks as hyperinflation peaked in 1923.

timeline

1873–96
The 'Great Deflation' follows the US Civil War

1920s
Germany suffers hyperinflation after the First World War

Different measures of inflation

CPI: The Consumer Price Index is the most common measure of inflation throughout the developed world, used everywhere from the United States, Europe and elsewhere. Statisticians calculate it by visiting shops and businesses throughout the country each month, checking how fast the price of an imaginary basket of goods and services has risen.

RPI: The Retail Price Index is used in the UK to measure the cost of living more comprehensively. It includes costs associated with home ownership, such as mortgage repayments and interest.

Gross domestic product deflator: This measure of prices – which is the most comprehensive of all – gauges the cost of all goods across the economy. However, it is produced far less regularly than the CPI and RPI figures.

PPI: The Producer Price Index measures both the cost of raw materials for manufacturers and the price they then charge retailers for their finished products. It is a useful signal of where inflation may be heading.

Other indices: There are many other more specific indices, including house-price indices and commodity-price measures.

Even lower inflation of around 20 per cent can be highly damaging – particularly when, as in the US and UK in the 1970s, it comes alongside weak economic growth or recession. The result is commonly known as stagflation (stagnant growth and high inflation), and in the US and UK it pushed up unemployment and bankruptcies for many years. Inflation, in short, has the power to wreck once proud and healthy economies.

Causes and effects Inflation tells us something about both social and economic conditions. By comparing how fast the cost of living is increasing with the speed at which households' incomes are rising, one can calculate the rate at which a society's standard of living is improving. If inflation outpaces families' wages, their standard of living is falling: people cannot afford to buy as many goods as they would otherwise have done. But when wages are rising faster than inflation, people have more money

1930

US and much of the world is trapped in deflation during the Great Depression

1970s

Oil crises usher in inflation of over 20 per cent in the US and UK

2008

In the face of hyperinflation, Zimbabwe issues the Z$100bn banknote in their pockets after paying for their weekly shopping bill: their standard of living improves.

When an economy is growing fast, employees receive generous pay increases, meaning they will spend more on goods and services. Prices will tend to rise in response to this increase in demand, whether it be for houses or haircuts. Likewise, if the economy slows, demand will follow suit and prices will come down, or will at least rise at a slower rate.

> **❝Inflation is the one form of taxation that can be imposed without legislation.❞**
> **Milton Friedman**

The price of goods is affected not just by demand but by the amount of money people have at their disposal. If the money supply grows (either because more money is printed or because banks are lending out more), there will be more money chasing the same volume of goods, which will push the price up. The debate over how precisely to influence this process was one of the major intellectual battles of the 20th century, between monetarists and Keynesians (see chapters 9 and 10).

Always inflation? A question frequently asked is whether prices always have to rise: can't they just stay still? In fact, they *can* freeze, and at various points in history have done so. Although inflation is not theoretically necessary for economies to function, politicians have tended, particularly in the past century or so, to encourage a little bit of inflation in their economies, for a number of reasons.

First, and most importantly, inflation encourages people to spend rather than save, because it slowly erodes the value of the money in one's pocket. A certain degree of this forward momentum is essential in modern capitalist economies, since in the long run it encourages companies to invest in new technologies. However, inflation also erodes debt, so indebted governments have in the past all too often allowed it to bubble ever higher, effectively reducing the amount of money they owe.

Similarly, inflation levels are usually analogous to interest rates (see chapter 18), and people are accustomed to positive rather than negative

> **The first panacea for a mismanaged nation is inflation of the currency; the second is war. Both bring a temporary prosperity; both bring a permanent ruin. But both are the refuge of political and economic opportunists.**
>
> Ernest Hemingway

interest rates. There have been few examples in history of banks charging customers to save and paying them to borrow (as would happen in a world of negative interest rates), and only in times of crisis when it was essential to encourage people to spend rather than save.

Finally, people are inherently used to rising wages. It is human nature – people strive to improve themselves, and often find it difficult to stomach a pay freeze each year, even if prices in the shops are more or less static.

Inflationary spirals Prices can sometimes rise exponentially in what is commonly called an inflationary spiral. The higher inflation goes, the more discontent it causes among workers, who see their standard of living deteriorating. They demand higher wages, and if they succeed they spend their extra cash, which in turn prompts shopkeepers to raise their prices. This pushes inflation still higher, which sends employees back to their bosses for more pay rises.

The fundamental problem with excessive inflation – or for that matter deflation (see chapter 20) – is that it can dangerously destabilize economies. When businesses and families feel insecure about how fast prices are rising or falling, they put off investing and saving, and normal life grinds to a halt. This is why governments and central banks are determined to keep prices ticking along at a predictable rate. Should they fail, then – as Ronald Reagan rightly pointed out – people are left to face a hugely unpleasant experience.

the condensed idea
Keep prices rising slowly

20 Debt and deflation

Unlike today, deflation – in which prices fall each year rather than rise – was not always seen as a threat. For a couple of hundred years up until the beginning of the 20th century, vibrant economies often experienced sustained bouts of the phenomenon. Indeed, Milton Friedman maintained that, in theory, governments should aim to sustain a moderate amount of deflation.

When prices of items on the high street and beyond are gently falling, it means that every pound or dollar you have in your pocket becomes worth more. Even if your income does not increase each year, its purchasing power does indeed go up. You need not worry, therefore, that your cash may become next to worthless in a few years' time, as could be the case in an economy with high inflation.

Definitions

Deflation implies that prices of goods and services are falling, usually on a year-to-year basis.
Disinflation is where the inflation rate slows down but remains positive.

Deflation and depression Benign deflation, however, was eclipsed in the 20th century by more painful experiences of falling prices – none more so than during the Great Depression of the 1930s. The Depression followed a major increase in share prices throughout the 1920s, with much of the stock bought not with savings but with borrowed cash. When in 1929 investors realized that the spectacular

timeline

1800s	1930
Industrial Revolution brings a sustained bout of deflation	The US suffers a debt-deflation spiral in the Great Depression

gains made (the Dow Jones Industrial Average had increased by a factor of five over the previous six years) were based not on reality but on hope and speculation, the market crashed.

What followed was the darkest period yet experienced by the US economy – and many other nations around the world – as banks collapsed under the weight of their debts, house prices fell, companies shut down and millions of people lost their jobs. One of the problems at the very core of the crisis was deflation.

Prices started to fall as people realized they had been artificially inflated by the greed and mania that had dominated the economy in the 'Roaring Twenties'. But although shares and house prices fell, the value of the debts people had taken on to secure them remained unchanged. So, with prices falling by 10 per cent a year, the cost of $100 of debt – in terms of what such a sum could now effectively purchase – rose to $110. Of those households that had not instantly succumbed to the crash, millions fell victim to deflation as the value of their debts arbitrarily increased.

A tougher spiral Deflation affects not only those with debts but the whole economy. As prices start to plummet, people tend to hoard cash, knowing that things will be cheaper in a few months. Their reluctance to spend causes prices to slide further. Furthermore, because people's salaries are usually set out in legally binding contracts, businesses suddenly find their wage bill effectively rising, as what was previously a $1,000 bill now costs the equivalent of $1,100. It is a disaster for the employer, who is selling goods and services for lower prices but still facing the same wage costs. And while it might initially seem good news for the employee, in practice it will mean companies having to fire more workers to keep themselves afloat. Similarly, although banks will receive increased mortgage payments from some borrowers – in relation to other prices in the economy, which are falling – other borrowers will not be able to pay them at all.

1990s	**2009**
Japan slumps into deflation as its property bubble bursts	Major economies, including the UK and US, experience deflation for the first time since the Second World War

> ❝I would emphasize the important corollary, of the debt-deflation theory, that great depressions are curable and preventable through reflation and stabilization.❞
>
> **Irving Fisher, US economist**

Many of these symptoms are very similar to those experienced in a period of high inflation. Both effectively involve the price of certain items rising, in real terms, at an uncontrollable rate. However, while inflation has the effect of making goods on the street more expensive, deflation inflates the cost of debt and other commitments.

The biggest risk with deflation is that prices fall at an ever-increasing rate as companies cut back and see their losses mount, which in turn will push prices lower still. This is arguably even more difficult to escape from than an inflationary spiral – largely because modern economies have evolved certain mechanisms to deal more effectively with the latter (see chapter 18).

Diagnosis and solutions The economic explanation for deflation is that the amount of money in the system falls or the supply of goods and services increases. So, whereas inflation involves too much money chasing too few goods, the opposite is true in deflation. In the case of the Great Depression and Japan's experience in the 1990s and 2000s, a contraction of money (associated with the debt bubble – when people saved more and spent less after years of excesses and living beyond their means) was the cause; the benign deflation of the 19th century was, in contrast, more a function of an increase in the supply of goods due to greater productivity.

Typically, the main tool central banks use to control inflation is interest rates. However, they cannot reduce these below zero, so when prices fall there is little more they can do except resort to more unconventional tools, most of which amount, in the words of Ben Bernanke, then a Federal Reserve Governor, to activating the 'printing presses'. In other

Deflation and the lost decade

Although the Great Depression is regarded as the worst deflationary spiral experienced in modern times – in the US, for example, unemployment rose to one-quarter of all able-bodied people and GDP shrank by a third – there have been other more recent recurrences of the phenomenon. The most notable was in Japan in the 1990s, where prices dropped into negative territory, forcing the Bank of Japan to cut interest rates to zero. The spiral contributed to a so-called 'lost decade' of anaemic growth and falling prices from which the country could not escape.

words, contrary to episodes of inflation when they attempt to keep the amount of cash in the economy constant, central banks start injecting more cash into the economy. They can do this a number of ways – for instance, by directly buying assets such as bonds or shares, or by increasing the amount of cash commercial banks have in their vaults – but all of them are known collectively as *quantitative easing*.

Such schemes were used by both the Japanese at the turn of the millennium, and the Federal Reserve and Bank of England after the 2008 financial crisis, as they attempted to reverse debt-fuelled financial crises. It remains to be seen whether their efforts will prove successful.

the condensed idea
Falling prices can cripple an economy

21 Taxes

'In this world nothing can be said to be certain except death and taxes,' said Benjamin Franklin in 1789. He was hardly the first person to complain about taxes. Ever since they came into existence governments have been devising ingenious ways of raising money. When Joseph and Mary travelled to Bethlehem, the Bible tells us, they were doing so to have their property registered for tax purposes; the Domesday Book Survey of England was ordered by William the Conqueror in 1086 largely in order to find out who he could tax; and as early as AD 10 Chinese citizens were having to pay an income tax.

Even today, taxes remain one of the most contentious issues in politics. President George H.W. Bush is still remembered today for his 1988 election pledge: 'Read my lips: no new taxes.' Sadly for him, the state of the public finances went against him, and so did the voters four years and several tax rises later.

> **'The hardest thing in the world to understand is the income tax.'**
> **Albert Einstein**

Since the dawn of history, people have resented having their hard-earned money taken from them – often with good reason. Tax collectors used to be far more brutal than they are now. In early days, peasants and labourers could expect to have to sell their wife or daughter into slavery if they couldn't afford to pay their taxes. Complaints about having to pay tax without having the right to influence policymaking in return (through, for example, the right to vote) triggered the signing of Magna Carta in 1215, the French Revolution and, of course, the Boston Tea Party and the American Revolutionary War.

timeline

3000BC
First evidence of taxation in Ancient Egypt

1789
The French Revolution begins, partly in opposition to high tax rates

However, in almost all of those instances, the taxes being levied were minuscule in comparison to those faced by citizens of most countries today. They were often no more than 10 per cent, and were occasional levies to pay for wars, which did not occur every year. Today, even Switzerland, which doesn't go to war, charges the average worker some 30 per cent of their salary in taxes.

The art of taxation What changed? Mainly the advent of the welfare state and social-security systems in the latter half of the 20th century. With states around the world suddenly committing themselves to pay for health, education, the welfare of the unemployed and elderly, and public safety, they had to spend a significant amount more than before, and so had to raise extra cash. Taxes were the answer.

And not merely *income taxes* (which deduct an amount based on someone's salary). Governments can now choose from a smorgasbord of taxation, with menu options including: *sales taxes* (also known as *ad valorem* taxes, levied on items at the point of purchase and including flat-rate excise on items like fuel); *capital gains taxes* (on profits from the sale of an investment that has increased in value); *business or corporation taxes* (on companies' profits); *inheritance taxes* (on the estate of someone who dies); *property taxes* (on home transactions); *import and export tariffs* (also known as customs duty); *environmental taxes* (on emissions); and *wealth taxes* (based on the value of one's assets).

In most countries both central state and local governments have the power to levy taxes. The local government tends to rely more on property taxes; central government on income taxes.

So, since the mid-20th century, tax systems have had the dual role of funding the institutions that protect citizens (the military, the police and emergency services, the courts and politicians) and redistributing wealth

1798

William Pitt the Younger introduces Britain's first income tax

1980s

Margaret Thatcher and Ronald Reagan mastermind major tax cuts in the UK and US

from those who can afford to spare it to those in need. And, typically, as a country grows richer the amount of tax it extracts from its citizens increases.

Smith's rules of taxation In *The Wealth of Nations* Adam Smith devised four rules for taxation:

1. *People should contribute in proportion to their income.* This means that those who earn more should pay more in taxes. Most countries operate a progressive tax system in which higher-income taxpayers actually pay a greater proportion of their income in taxes than poorer ones. They face higher tax rates as well as a higher tax bill. Taxes can also be proportional (including flat taxes, where everyone pays the same rate) or regressive (where rich people pay a smaller proportion of their earnings or wealth). Typically, in today's progressive income tax systems people receive a tax-free allowance. Then they pay a certain percentage on another part of their salary up to a certain level, then an even higher proportion on the next tranche, and so on.
2. *Tax should be certain, not arbitrary, with the time and manner of payment clear to all.*

Ricardian equivalence

The Ricardian Equivalence theory (named after David Ricardo, the economist behind Comparative Advantage, see chapter 7) suggests that governments should not fund tax cuts by borrowing money.

Cutting taxes is often seen as a good way to boost the economy: it leaves people with more money in their pockets, which they should theoretically go out and spend. However, if tax cuts are funded by government borrowing then, according to some economists, they can have little effect, since they will only be temporary, having to be paid back in the future through higher taxes or lower government spending. Although this law of Ricardian Equivalence undermines the case for so-called 'unfunded' tax cuts, it has rarely prevented politicians from going ahead with them.

3. *Tax should come at a convenient time.* For instance, taxes on rents should be payable when rents are due.

4. *Taxes should cost no more than necessary – both to the citizen and the state.* In other words, they should interfere as little as possible in the choices people make in their everyday lives. It is all too easy to discourage people from working more hours by increasing the marginal rate of tax (i.e. the rate someone would pay if they worked an hour more than they do currently). However, this is an area of major debate, since some argue that the tax system should be used as a tool to encourage citizens to do certain 'good' things and discourage them from others. For example, most governments levy high taxes on cigarettes and alcohol for reasons of public health.

> '**The art of taxation consists in so plucking the goose as to get the most feathers with the least hissing.**'
>
> Jean-Baptiste Colbert, French minister of finance (1665–83)

The limits of taxation The higher taxes are, the greater the incentive people have to avoid them. This is the experience many governments around the world faced in the 1970s and 1980s. Some workers faced marginal tax rates – in other words the tax rate they paid on every extra dollar or pound of income they earned – of 70 per cent or higher. Rather than working the extra hours, they tended to work less, or avoided paying the tax by putting their extra income into their pensions or by moving their cash to tax havens overseas. In an age where money can be transferred anywhere in the world at the press of a button, preventing the latter has become highly difficult, with the result that most governments have little choice but to keep their taxes as competitive as possible.

Nonetheless, over time taxes have tended to build up and accrete one upon the other, making the system more complex and intransigent with every year that passes. Tellingly, when William Pitt the Younger introduced Britain's first income tax in 1798, he insisted it was only a temporary measure to pay for the Napoleonic Wars. Perhaps he even meant it at the time!

the condensed idea
As inevitable as death

22 Unemployment

In economics, everything finally comes back to unemployment. However much attention the experts and politicians pay to a country's gross domestic product, inflation, interest rates or wealth, the simple question of whether people do or do not have jobs remains central. The objective of full employment is usually one of the first manifesto pledges made by political parties around the world – though the extent to which they stick to such a promise can vary wildly.

Governments' resolve to tackle unemployment is understandable, given the trauma associated with losing one's job, yet it is the ability of companies to hire and fire as they evolve that makes the free market such a dynamic way to run an economy. If a real-estate agent sees its business drying up amid a housing slump, it can try to economize by cutting back on marketing or office costs, but these are as nothing compared with the savings it can make by laying off staff. It is the interplay between these two forces – the government's desire to see as many people in work as possible and companies' need to stay afloat – that shapes not just the labour market but the fate of the wider economy.

A tale of two labour markets Compare the experience of Europe and the United States. In most of Europe, labour-market laws restrict a company's ability to fire its workers and ensure that it pays employees a minimum wage. But, as US Economist Thomas Sowell put it in his work *Basic Economics*, 'Job security policies save the jobs of existing workers, but at the cost of reducing the flexibility and efficiency of the economy as a whole, thereby inhibiting the creation of new jobs for other workers.'

timeline

1933

Unemployment in the US hits 25 per cent during the Great Depression

Unemployment pays

All too often governments can actually encourage people to remain unemployed by making their unemployment insurance more attractive than it ought to be.

A study by Harvard economist Martin Feldstein showed that for some people it pays not to have a job. Consider someone who could work for $10 an hour or collect unemployment benefit of $8 an hour. On the benefit they pay tax of 18 per cent, and so receive $6.56 after this has been deducted. If that person were working, he or she would pay 18 per cent income tax and 7.5 per cent in social security contributions, leaving him or her with a net salary of $7.45. Comparing this with what they would receive if they claimed benefit, one may well decide that a day of leisure is worth more than the extra 89 cents an hour the job would pay. Governments are constantly trying to strike a balance between encouraging people to get back into work and compensating them for losing their jobs.

Because of this, Europe has tended to create jobs at a far slower rate than the United States, where the labour market is significantly more flexible.

Definition of unemployment In its very broadest sense unemployment simply means the state of not having a job. However, for economists this is an inadequate definition. There is a big difference between a temporary office worker who is merely between jobs for a few weeks ('frictional unemployment') and a factory mechanic whose skills are no longer in demand because his industry has moved most of its production overseas. The former will soon be back in work contributing to private-sector economic output; the latter may need to be retrained, often at the expense of the state over a significant period of time.

1970s	**1979**
Unemployment rises sharply in the face of oil shocks	Conservative Party is voted into power in the UK following an advertising campaign proclaiming: 'Labour Isn't Working'

Unemployment rates

(percentage of working population) at the end of 2008

France 7.9

United States 7.6

Germany 7.2

United Kingdom 6.3

Japan 3.9

Source: Office for National Statistics

To try to distinguish between different situations, economists have devised various classifications of unemployment. According to the International Labour Organization (ILO) the strict definition of unemployment is when someone is out of work but actively seeking to get back into the labour market. The percentage of workers in the US who met this description in 2008 was 6.5 per cent, compared with 5.6 per cent in the UK and 7 per cent in the European Union. There is another category for those who are long-term unemployed, which is usually a far bigger proportion (at 21 per cent in the UK) since it includes students, pensioners, stay-at-home mothers and those who are too sick or disabled to work. Economists also distinguish between the ages of those who are employed – and with good reason. Studies show that if you are out of a job for a long period in your teens or early twenties you are much more likely to slip into the ranks of the long-term or permanently unemployed thereafter.

Measures of joblessness There are two ways to measure unemployment. The traditional way is to count the number of people claiming unemployment benefits. The problem with this is that not everyone who is out of work and looking for a job will claim these payments – often for reasons of pride, occasionally due to apathy, and sometimes because they suspect they are not eligible. The modern, and arguably more comprehensive, way to measure unemployment is to survey a representative slice of the population – in the UK this consists of 60,000 people from all backgrounds – on their current working situation.

Unemployment levels tend to ebb and flow along with the wider economy. In the United States during the Great Depression they hit levels of 25 per cent. However, the jobless rate never drops to zero. In fact, for all governments' good intentions about bringing down unemployment, the rate has rarely dipped beneath 4 per cent of the working population, even when the economy has been powering ahead.

In practice, full employment is impossible, partly because people need time to seek out the right job even when it's available and partly because, as an economy develops and technology advances, some workers will inevitably lack the skills necessary to take on particular jobs. Often, unemployment is higher than it would otherwise be because, owing to minimum-wage laws or the wage-bargaining power of unions, firms have to pay their workers higher wages than they can strictly afford. Similarly, the existence of unemployment benefit can encourage some to remain unemployed rather than work. Countries therefore have what economists call 'the natural rate of unemployment' – quite simply, the long-run average unemployment rate.

One of Britain's most famous economists, A.W. Phillips, detected an uncanny relationship between unemployment levels and inflation. If unemployment falls below a certain level, it will push wages, and hence inflation, higher as companies become prepared to pay more to get hold of staff. The opposite is true with high unemployment, which tends to push down inflation. In economic parlance, there is a negative correlation between inflation and unemployment. Phillips's theory gave birth to one of the most enduring models in economics – the Phillips Curve, which graphically illustrates this negative correlation. If you want to keep unemployment at, say, 4 per cent, then – it shows – you will have to settle for inflation of 6 per cent. If you want to restrict inflation to 2 per cent, you will have to accept an unemployment level of 7 per cent.

Together with Edmund Phelps, renowned economist Milton Friedman took this idea a step further, devising the theory of the 'non-accelerating inflation rate of unemployment' (NAIRU). The thrust of this is that although policymakers can follow the Phillips Curve to bring down unemployment in the short run, eventually unemployment will creep back up towards its natural rate (meanwhile efforts to boost the economy by cutting interest rates will generate extra inflation, but that's another story).

Politicians still promise people more jobs and higher employment than is realistic. However, it is up to economists to come up with the dismal retort that full employment is practically impossible.

> **'Probably the single most important macroeconomic relationship is the Phillips Curve.'**
> **George Akerlof, Nobel Prize-winning economist**

the condensed idea
Zero unemployment is impossible

23 Currencies and exchange rates

Some years ago, experts at the Federal Reserve in Washington DC put together a model designed to predict future trends in the world's major currencies. They had access to more information on foreign-exchange markets than economists in any other country and they were confident of success. For months they worked on the project until, at last, it was time to switch on the machine . . .

Days later it was clear that the experiment was a complete flop. According to the then Fed Chairman, Alan Greenspan, 'The rate of return on that investment of time and effort and people was zero.' Such a result was perhaps unsurprising. The foreign-exchange markets attract trillions of dollars of speculative investment every year as people try to second-guess currency movements. But they are arguably the most volatile and unpredictable of all markets.

All of us become currency speculators of a sort, when we travel abroad. As soon as we swap dollars or pounds for pesos or euros we are investing in a foreign currency, the value of which is likely to rise or fall by the time we arrive back home.

Currency markets Currency markets, often known as Forex (short for foreign exchange), are where investors buy and sell currencies. They are among the world's oldest financial institutions, stretching back to Roman times and before, and have existed for as long as there has been money and

timeline

1944
Bretton Woods agreement

1966
Bretton Woods starts to break down

The euro and currency unions

The most famous currency union, whereby different countries share a single currency, is the euro – the 15-member currency union in Europe (as of 2008). Preceded by the European Exchange Rate Mechanism (ERM), which ensured prospective members kept their economies in lock-step with each other, the euro was introduced fully in 2002, replacing each member state's currency.

Past attempts at other currency systems had collapsed as national governments sought independence in economic policy, but the Euro's founders tackled this by creating one central bank to set interest rates for the entire euro area, and an agreement over the limits within which governments can borrow and spend.

More recently, there have been talks between countries in, respectively, the Persian Gulf and Latin America about possible currency unions.

international trade. But the Romans would reel at the size, sophistication and international breadth of the markets that have evolved today.

Every year trillions of dollars' (or euros', or pounds') worth of currency is bought and sold by investors. Sometimes those investors will be companies, keen to ensure their profits are not obliterated if, for instance, the strength of the dollar leaps, making their imports from the United States much more expensive. They are seeking currency hedges in order to insure themselves against risk. At times they are governments, intervening in the currency markets to ensure their own currency remains at a certain level. At other times they are investors and hedge-fund managers with a hunch that a currency is about to take a tumble. And sometimes they are merely foreign tourists like you and me.

Rises and falls There are many reasons why a currency rises and falls, but two in particular affect its behaviour. First, and most importantly, a currency tends to rise and fall in tandem with perceptions of the economic health of the country with which it's associated (or the jurisdiction that issues that currency).

1979	2002	2005
Introduction of the European Exchange Rate Mechanism	Full introduction of the euro	China loosens its peg on its currency, the renminbi

Second, currency investors tend to chase the currency with the highest yield. If a country has high interest rates it means the government bonds and other investment opportunities it issues will offer a greater return than in a country with very low interest rates. Investors from around the world buy them up, and as a result of this extra demand for the country's investments, the value of the currency increases. In contrast, the currency falls if rates are low and people abandon their investments denominated in that currency.

Floating or pegged? Since the 1970s almost every country in the Western world has had a floating currency, the value of which ebbs and flows against other currencies as determined by the markets. However, there are notable exceptions, with some countries fixing their currencies against either another currency or a group of them. The most renowned example is China, whose government carefully controls the value of the renminbi against the dollar by buying dollar-denominated assets as necessary.

> ❛**The dollar may be our currency but it's your problem.**❜
>
> **John Connally, Nixon's Secretary of the Treasury, to European central bankers**

Other nations occasionally intervene by doing the same if they believe their currency is over- or undervalued. Japan and the euro area have both done so since the turn of the millennium. There is considerable evidence that it is highly beneficial for vulnerable, emerging nations to fix their currencies in this way, since it improves stability, encourages people to invest and helps trade relations.

Floating rates were not the norm in the world until relatively recently. Throughout much of the 19th and 20th centuries, governments kept the rate of their currencies fixed. In the times of the Gold Standard, they fixed the values of their currencies against the amount of gold they had in their vaults. The idea was that gold is a universal currency, of equal value anywhere in the world.

The system improved global trade, since businesses did not have to worry about how the rise or fall of currencies in countries to which they were exporting would affect their profits. The problem was that the amount of gold being mined could not keep pace with the growth of trade and investment. The Gold Standard eventually became a major restraint on fast-growing economies, and was abandoned by many around the time of the Great Depression.

Bretton Woods After the Second World War, a group of economists and policymakers met in the smart Mount Washington Hotel in the US town of Bretton Woods, New Hampshire, to devise a new system for regulating international exchange rates. They came up with a fixed-rate system, this time aligned to the US dollar, since the US by that stage was clearly the world's economic superpower, and the dollar happened to be stable, its value fixed against gold. Each country pledged to *peg* its currency – in other words, to ensure it remained equal to a certain number of dollars.

The problem with fixing a currency against another, however, is that the country in question loses some of its ability to control its economy. When one country in a currency union raises its interest rates the rest have to do so as well, or risk setting off a major inflationary spiral. The Bretton Woods arrangement started to break down in 1966, but, as we shall see, it was not the last of the major currency systems.

Currency speculation Some argue that fixed exchange-rate systems can mask the true value of a currency, and there have been many examples in recent years when speculators launched assaults on a country's currency – selling it off in the belief that the pegs were unsustainable. This happened to various Asian countries during the financial crisis of the late 1990s and, even more notoriously, to sterling. On 'Black Wednesday' in September 1992, the UK was forced to abandon its brief membership of the ERM (European Exchange Rate Mechanism) after speculators, led by hedge-fund billionaire George Soros, attacked it. Despite raising interest rates to double-digit levels, the UK Treasury was unable to prevent an exodus of investors from the pound, and eventually it surrendered, allowing the pound to depreciate (fall) against other currencies around the world. It was a traumatic day for the UK economy, and encapsulates precisely how directly a currency's level reflects perceptions of a country's economic policies.

the condensed idea
The barometer of a country's standing

24 Balance of payments

Until relatively recently, few aspects of economic news were as eagerly awaited as the balance of payments statistics. The details of a country's financial and economic interaction with the rest of the world were regarded as among the most important in assessing its health, alongside its gross domestic product. Although we are no longer as obsessed by balance of payments statistics as we once were, they remain the ultimate guide to a country's international economic relations.

Given that the balance of payments accounts for all the trade that flows into and out of a country, including money injected into it from overseas nations or, for instance, sent out to families and business counterparts living in foreign countries, its importance can hardly be overstated. The balance of payments shows whether a country is borrowing and over-extending itself over a period of time – potentially storing up trouble for the future – or lending out cash to others in exchange for goods. Ultimately, it will reveal whether a country has a prosperous future ahead of it or, conversely, whether it will have to seek help from, say, the International Monetary Fund in order to stay afloat.

Current and capital accounts The balance of payments is made up of two main parts: the current and the capital accounts.

• *The current account* The current account measures the flow of goods and services into and out of a country. These are often called visible trade

timeline

1901– 32	1944
The Gold Standard still employed	The Bretton Woods Agreement on fixed exchange rates

(physical goods) and invisible trade (cash paid for services such as legal advice, advertising, architecture and so on). If a country imports significantly more goods and services than it exports, it will have a large current account deficit. Since the 1980s the US and the UK have operated large current account deficits almost every year, as they have invariably imported more than they have exported to the rest of the world. Countries with large current account surpluses, on the other hand, have been major exporters: Germany and Japan, historically, and, more recently, China, which has earned the label as the world's

A different type of deficit

The balance of payments records the financial and economic flows between one country and other parts of the world over a given period – usually a quarter or a year. It includes both the public or state sector and the private sector, and should not be confused with the budget or fiscal accounts, which record a government's spending and borrowing.

workshop because of the massive quantity of goods it sends out around the world. Also included in the account are any unilateral transfers in money overseas, for instance foreign aid and gifts, as well as cash sent by workers to families overseas.

• *The capital account* Although a country can have a deficit in its current account, this has necessarily to be balanced out elsewhere (hence balance of payments). If Japan sells a million dollars' worth of cars to the Americans, it will then be left with those dollars and will need to spend them, either on American investments or by putting them in US bank accounts. So, for instance, China, which throughout the 1990s and 2000s has had a massive surplus on its trade with the US and other Western countries, has used this dollar mountain to buy trillions of dollars' worth of US investments – everything from government debt to shares in major companies.

Harmless deficits A current account deficit, which typically comes hand in hand with a trade deficit, indicates that a country is borrowing

1970s	**1998**	**2008**
Richard Nixon abandons Bretton Woods	Russia faces a balance of payments crisis and is forced to default on sovereign debt	Iceland, Ukraine and Latvia are among countries forced to seek IMF assistance

from other nations in order to fund itself, its appetite for consumption having outweighed its ability to produce goods to satisfy its demands. This might appear somewhat worrying, but it need not be – in small measures at least. Some degree of current account deficit can be an entirely healthy phenomenon in a country.

Throughout the 1980s, and again in the early 2000s, much publicity surrounded the American current account deficit, which swung to a record high of 6 per cent of gross domestic product – over three-quarters of a trillion dollars. The UK was burdened with a similar-sized percentage deficit.

Some warned that the countries might experience a full-blown balance of payments crisis. This happens when one part of the balance of payments – generally the current account – cannot be funded by the other. This has happened a number of times, for instance in the Asian financial crisis in the late 1990s and in Russia at the same time. These countries had large current account deficits and, as investors around the world realized that they were heading for a major slide, they started refusing to buy anything denominated in roubles, baht and so on. It meant that the capital account could no longer balance out the current account deficit. Such circumstances inevitably entail a serious and inescapable economic crisis.

Balancing the accounts

If a country has a deficit in its current account it must be evened out by an equal surplus in its capital account, which measures cash spent on investments overseas and cash earned from existing investments. So, for instance, Britons and British companies tend to earn a significant amount off their foreign investments, which slightly offsets the country's sizable current account deficit.

The only way a country can afford to import more goods than it exports is if other countries are willing to buy up assets denominated in its currency, whether it be dollars, pounds or pesos.

'Our country has been behaving like an extraordinarily rich family that possesses an immense farm. In order to consume 4 per cent more than we produce ... we have, day by day, been both selling pieces of the farm and increasing the mortgage on what we still own ...'
Warren Buffett

However, most deficits can be safely sustained for many years. What usually ensues when a country runs a large current account deficit is not a crisis but a decline in its currency's value against others. As the exchange rate drops the nation's exports become cheaper and therefore more attractive to foreigners; this, in turn, boosts that country's sales abroad, which should bring down the current account deficit. So, in an international system of floating exchange rates, current account deficits are inevitable, but they are also supposed to be self-correcting.

Keeping an eye on deficits This is not always the case. As mentioned in the previous chapter, at various points in history there have been fixed exchange-rate systems, most famously, the Gold Standard in the 19th and earlier 20th centuries, followed by the Bretton Woods system of fixed exchange rates from 1945 to the 1970s. During these periods, countries running current account deficits had to slow down their economies in order to bring them back into balance. Politicians and economists would scrutinize the balance of payments statistics to detect whether they augured well or ill for the economy.

Even if the world does not move back to a system of fixed exchange rates, it remains important to monitor whether countries have deficits or surpluses in their current accounts, and to identify the structure of their balance of payments – such statistics provide a yardstick for a nation's future prosperity.

the condensed idea
The ledger of a country's international economic relations

25 Trust and the law

How heavy is a kilogram? That may seem an odd question: most of us know what it feels like to pick up something weighing a kilo, or for that matter a pound or stone. However, there is only one object in the world that officially weighs precisely one kilogram, and it sits in a guarded vault just outside Paris, France. The International Prototype Kilogram, a small cylinder of platinum and iridium made in 1889, is the object against which all scales in the world are calibrated.

The lump of metal is heavily guarded since many fear that if it were damaged or went missing, business around the globe would grind to a halt. A company buying a tonne of steel from factories on the other side of the world could no longer be certain it was receiving the correct amount and not being short-changed through the use of inaccurately calibrated scales.

Setting standards The economy cannot function to the best of its capability without official standards, set down in law both nationally and around the world. Moreover, even the most ardent free marketers – who believe that just about every business out there, from central banks to power companies and road planners, should be privatized – accept that we still need governments to enforce legal and property rights. Without such laws the free market could not properly function and we would be left instead with anarchy – a danger that Adam Smith, the father of economics, pointed out back in the 18th century.

timeline

AD529	1100–1200
Byzantine Emperor Justinian lays down the foundations of modern civil law in his *Corpus Juris Civilis*	Common law system originates in medieval England

We need governments to enforce contracts between people and businesses and to set down standards that citizens should follow. People need to be secure in the knowledge that if they own something it will not be arbitrarily confiscated, and that cheating and stealing will not go unpunished.

Capitalism is highly reliant on trust. When a bank lends money to someone, its judgement over whether to hand out the cash is partly based on whether they trust that individual will be able to pay it back. Similarly, a country can afford to run up large amounts of debt provided international investors believe it will not default in the future.

One party in a transaction not only needs to trust the other party; it also needs to trust the structure that frames the transaction. Thus, a government's paramount role is not providing social welfare, determining interest rates or redistributing wealth – it is enshrining a stable and fair system of property and other legal rights through which it can hold accountable those who break their laws.

One of the prime reasons Britain thrived throughout the years of the Industrial Revolution was because its legal system was regarded as highly dependable. This was in stark contrast to many of its European counterparts, where wars and disputes often threw property rights into question – to the extent that landowners could never be sure whether they really had full ownership of their property, and could not rely on the state to back them should they be wronged.

Intellectual property rights It is not just the rights to solid, visible property that need to be protected; ownership of invisible property such as ideas and artistic creations also requires protection. An inventor has little incentive to innovate if he knows that his invention will be seized from him – depriving him of any reward for his work – as soon as it is finished.

1700–1800

Commercial law starts to
be written into national
law systems

late 1900s

Creation of the European
Union establishes new layer
of law in Europe

Shantytown property rights

Are the poor really as poor as we think they are? Peruvian economist Hernando de Soto has argued that many of the world's poorest families are so merely because they do not have legal rights to their property. A family may have lived in the same small shack in the favelas near Rio for years, but because only informal property and legal rights have been developed among the poor they are at the mercy of local criminals and vigilantes (who may attempt to steal or destroy their home) or the government (which may attempt to drive the shantytown dwellers elsewhere).

The solution, de Soto has argued, is to give these people legal rights to their properties. That way they will not only have an incentive to take more care of them, but will also be able to borrow cash by using their homes as a guarantee. He argues that the total value of homes owned by the poor in the developing world is more than 90 times the total foreign aid given to these countries in the past 30 years.

So, for an economy to function properly, governments have to ensure it has a stable system of patents and other intellectual property rights. Copyright, for example, protects writers for a set period of time against plagiarism.

Intellectual property rights have come under great scrutiny in recent years thanks to the rise of emerging economies such as China and India. In such countries, regulations and laws on intellectual property and common standards have proven hard to uphold. As a result, companies have been able to produce, for example, cheap and unlicensed versions of drugs based on the research and development of Western pharmacological companies. Although consumers initially welcomed such projects, there have subsequently been several scares over whether goods produced in these countries can be trusted. For instance, some counterfeit drugs produced in China have turned out to have no effect, or to be actually harmful.

File sharing The intellectual property debate has reached fever pitch in recent years, since modern technology has made it easy to spread intangible ideas very quickly. Within minutes of switching on your computer you can illicitly download an mp3 of a chart song or a recently released movie. The singer or cast get no cash, and you get your entertainment for free – so, bearing in mind the economic rule that there is no such thing as a free lunch, who actually pays for this?

The answer is that we all do – albeit indirectly. As artists receive less income, they have less incentive to produce further material; fewer people are drawn towards the industry, and eventually the quality of music and films in the marketplace deteriorates. Conventional economics would argue strongly that governments have a duty to ensure that such piracy happens as little as possible, though others claim that many artists are sufficiently well paid to stomach a little less in royalties.

The tragedy of the commons Poor or insufficient property rights can greatly damage an economy. Granting people legal ownership rights frees them to invest more in their property, in the hope of adding to its value. You are far more likely to spend some cash and time painting your apartment if you own it, as opposed to merely squatting in it. The alternative scenario is the 'tragedy of the commons' – a situation where people abuse a resource because they do not own it (see chapter 1).

When Western economists visited the Soviet Union during communism they discovered that despite the country suffering major food crises, farmers would allow their fertile land to lie fallow, and crops to waste in the fields or warehouses. The problem was that under a communist system they had no direct property rights over their crops, and so far less incentive to work the fields harder and produce more food. Part of the reason that vast stretches of northern Africa are deserts is not merely because of climate or soil conditions – with some hard work and investment such areas could be returned to grassland. It is because the land is used by nomads and their herds, who have little incentive to look after the land as after a while they will move on. The result is often overgrazing.

Governments, then, must ensure not only that people respect their laws and contracts, but also that they put in place the right laws to ensure people contribute to a thriving economy. At the same time, they must ensure that certain inalienable standards – of weights, lengths and other measures – remain in place.

the condensed idea
The irreplaceable foundations of society

26 Energy and oil

All kinds of commodities matter to the global economy. Without steel or concrete the world's construction industries would grind to a halt, while the electrical grids that give us our power supply are dependent on copper wire. However, no commodity has been as important – or occasionally as troublesome – over the past century as crude oil.

Three times in the past fifty years oil prices have jumped sharply, pushing up the cost of living significantly throughout the developed world. The first two price rises happened for largely political reasons, while the third was chiefly due to economic forces, but each time the price spike forced politicians to ask searching questions about humankind's complex relationship with its sources of energy.

This relationship is hardly a new one. Since prehistoric times people have used natural resources to enhance their existence – first through the burning of wood and peat for survival. Then, in the Industrial Revolution, coal was burnt to produce steam power. In the 20th century, other carbon-based fossil fuels (so called because they come from the fossilized remains of dead plants and animals in the earth's crust) such as oil and natural gas became key sources of energy. So ingrained has the use of petroleum-based products become in modern society that it is easy to forget there would be no cars or air travel without them, and the vast majority of our power stations would close down. But nor is oil used only for energy; 16 per cent of our usage goes into making plastics, together with various pharmaceuticals, solvents, fertilizers and pesticides.

OPEC and the first two oil crises Although developed countries such as the United States, United Kingdom and Norway have extensive

timeline

1900s

Private motoring becomes more popular, thus dramatically increasing demand for oil

No ordinary commodity

Like other commodities, such as corn or gold, oil (and natural gas, which is closely related and behaves in a similar way) is an asset that can be traded on a futures market (see chapter 30), and its price goes up and down when supply and demand rise and fall. However, energy commodities are different for two main reasons.

First, energy is so important to the functioning of a state that politicians tend to view energy security as a matter of national security, and when politicians get involved in something then the usual assumptions about supply,

demand and price tend no longer to apply.

Second, it is only in recent years that energy prices have started to reflect the long-term costs to society of pollution. Burning fossil fuels emits a cocktail of gases, which most scientists believe are directly linked to global warming. Such indirect repercussions of an activity, where people can cause harm or expensive damage to innocent bystanders without having to pay or answer for it, are something economists call 'externalities' (see chapter 45).

oil reserves, a far greater proportion of the world's oil is to be found in the Middle East and a number of other volatile political areas. Chief among them is Saudi Arabia, which has a fifth of the world's known reserves. In the 1970s, in response to a number of political issues in the Middle East, producers with large reserves banded together to form the Organization of Petroleum Exporting Countries (OPEC). This was designed as a cartel – that is, a group of sellers collaborating to control prices. Between 1973 and 1975 they shut down much of their production, and the resulting lack of global supply doubled the oil price.

As a result, inflation in the US jumped into double-digits and economic growth stalled, leaving the country, and a number of other Western nations, facing stagflation (see chapter 19). Unemployment in the US rose from 4.9 per cent to 8.5 per cent during the same period.

The same happened again in the early 1980s, with even more dire consequences, since on this occasion the Federal Reserve, under Chairman

1973–75	**early 1980s**	**2007–8**
First oil crisis	Second oil crisis	Oil prices soar to record highs, but drop sharply as a global recession begins

Paul Volcker, attempted to fight the rise in inflation with high interest rates, pushing unemployment levels up beyond 10 per cent. The crisis eventually abated following political negotiation with the Saudis, while at the same time OPEC was hit by economic reality: fewer buyers of oil meant less revenue for OPEC, so members of the cartel began pumping more than their stated allowance to try to raise their incomes.

A third oil crisis? Between the early years of this millennium and 2008, oil prices increased in value seven times. In real terms (in other words after inflation is taken into account) they rose past the peak they hit in the 1970s. However, whereas the previous crises were specifically political, generated by the actions of OPEC, this one was more speculative in nature.

> ❛We have a serious problem: America is addicted to oil, which is often imported from unstable parts of the world.❜
>
> President George W. Bush

Investors, such as hedge-fund managers, bought up millions of barrels of oil, suspecting that its price would continue to soar higher still. Part of their rationale was that China and other fast-growing countries would demand significant amounts of oil in the coming years; another justification was that oil is a finite resource which could, at some point in the future, run out. Indeed, many believe that oil production has passed its peak, and that in years to come it will no longer be possible to produce as much oil as previously. If such a theory is true, countries will either have to find new sources of energy or accept an inevitable decline in their standards of living.

The fact that terrorists were increasingly targeting oil rigs and refineries in the Middle East, Nigeria and elsewhere in the wake of the invasion of Iraq and the overthrow of Saddam Hussein in 2003 gave prospective buyers another reason to fret about supply. Meanwhile, on the other side of the supply/demand equation, the rapid rise of China and other fast-growing developing nations meant that demand for energy hit record levels. The combined effect was to push up the price of oil to just under $150 a barrel in the first half of 2008.

Higher oil prices again pushed up inflation across the world, but the global financial crisis of the time brought about a major economic downturn, which quickly pushed oil prices back down to below $40 a barrel by the end of the year.

Although the developed world continues to consume record amounts of oil – in terms of number of barrels – the amount of oil it needs to generate an extra dollar of economic growth has diminished since the 1970s. According to the US Department of Energy, energy consumption per dollar of gross domestic product has declined at an average annual rate of 1.7 per cent over the past quarter-century.

Alternative energy The energy shocks of the 1970s prompted companies and governments to seek new ways of becoming energy efficient, and of reducing reliance on oil. Car producers devised ways of making engines run for more miles on less fuel – particularly in Japan and Europe, where high fuel taxes already made efficiency an attractive goal. A number of countries increasingly turned to nuclear power – despite a temporary plunge in its use following the 1986 Chernobyl disaster. They also began to look at other sources of energy that do not rely directly on fossil fuels. Most Western countries, for example, have now developed small but growing schemes to generate solar, wind, wave or geothermal energy. In the wake of the recent energy crisis, the quest for alternative technologies has intensified, with major car producers building hybrid and fully electric cars that can be recharged from mains electricity.

Although many of these technologies are still at a nascent stage, their adoption shows how even in an inelastic market (that is, one where consumers cut back relatively slowly in response to price rises), slowly but surely humans adapt and change their behaviour when the balance between supply and demand shifts.

the condensed idea
Deal with oil shortages through innovation

27 Bond markets

'I used to think that, if there was such a thing as reincarnation, I wanted to come back as the president, or the pope, or a .400 baseball hitter,' said James Carville, campaign manager to former US President Bill Clinton. 'But now I want to come back as the bond market. You intimidate everybody.'

The international bond markets where companies and governments raise money are far less renowned and understood than their equity counterpart – the stock market – yet they are in many respects far more important and influential. By determining whether a country can cheaply raise cash or not, the bond markets have helped determine the course of wars, revolutions and political struggles, and have had far-reaching implications in almost every corner of life for centuries. Even in times of peace, the ability of a government to raise money is of massive importance to a country's citizens: the higher the interest rates it has to pay, the higher are the borrowing costs all the way across the economy. So ignore the bond market at your peril.

The price of sovereign bonds (bonds issued by a national government) reveals how creditworthy a government is, how easy it finds it to raise cash, and how its policies are regarded. If a government is no longer able to tap the bond market it will struggle to survive at all.

A bond is essentially a type of IOU which promises to pay the owner a certain lump sum at a point in the future, as well as a stream of interest payments throughout the bond's life – usually at annual intervals. A typical government bond, for, say $100,000, will last for anything from a couple of years to half a century, and will pay a nominal – in other words

timeline

face-value – interest rate fixed at around 4–5 per cent. Once the bonds have been issued they can be traded on the massive international bond markets to be found in financial centres from New York to London and Tokyo.

The rate's the thing The real power of bond markets lies in the fact that the interest rate the markets determine for the bond can be quite different from that advertised on the bond itself. If investors believe a government is (a) at risk of defaulting or (b) likely to push up inflation (which in many senses is also a kind of default, since inflation erodes value), they will tend to sell off that government's bonds. This has the double effect of pushing down the price of the bond and pushing up the actual rate of interest it pays out.

This makes economic sense: the riskier an asset is, the less investors should pay for it, and the greater should be the compensation for holding it (the interest rate).

Suppose there is a $10,000 US Treasury bond with a 4.5 per cent interest rate (also known as its yield). For the duration of its life (it could be 10 years, 20 years or more) it will pay out $450 to its holder each year. For anyone who buys the bond at its offer price this represents a 4.5 per cent interest rate. But what if investors get jittery about the creditworthiness of the US government and start selling their bonds? The price drops to $9,000. At this price, that $450 yield is actually worth 5 per cent to new investors.

> **"I don't care a damn about stocks and bonds, but I don't want to see them go down the first day I am President."**
>
> **Theodore Roosevelt**

The market rate of bonds is highly important since it influences the rates at which a government can issue future bonds and still hope to find buyers. If it is to find buyers for the thousands of bonds it issues weekly, it must adapt the initial interest rates (the coupon rate) to the market rate on existing bonds. The higher the rates it has to pay, the harder it becomes to

1815

Nathan Rothschild makes a fortune on the bond market after the Battle of Waterloo

1914

Turmoil after bond markets fail to predict the start of the First World War

1998

Bond prices soar after hedge-fund Long-Term Capital Management collapses

From AAA to C ratings

Bonds – whether they are issued by a country or a company – are regarded as among the safest investments available. When a company collapses, the bondholders are closest to the front of the queue to have their investment paid back, while shareholders have to wait until later, when much of the cash may already have been paid out. However, the possibility of default is a key consideration for investors, and as a result a complex apparatus has been constructed to guide them as to the safety or otherwise of any particular bond. Credit-ratings agencies, such as Standard & Poors or Moody's and Fitch, exist to rate government and corporate bonds based on the likelihood of default. These ratings range from AAA, the best quality, to C. Typically, bonds rated at BAA or above are regarded as 'investment grade' and those below are called 'junk bonds'. In recompense for the higher risk of default, the junk bonds' interest rates are usually far higher.

borrow and the more it is forced to cut back. It is little wonder that James Carville found the market so intimidating.

Since governments throughout the world typically have to borrow in order to keep their budgets balanced (see chapter 38) they are regularly issuing new bonds. In the US, the most common types of government bonds are known as Treasury bills, Treasury notes and Treasury bonds. In the UK, they are known as gilt-edged securities, or gilts, because the government is regarded as a highly reliable creditor.

Origins of bonds Bonds originated in medieval Italy, where the city states, often at war with one another, would force their wealthier citizens to lend them certain amounts in exchange for regular interest payments. Although modern investors are not forced to buy bonds, in the US and UK the bulk of government debt is owned by the citizens, largely through their pension funds. Pension funds are obliged to put a major chunk of their cash into government debt, since it is regarded as the least risky investment available.

It was not until the Napoleonic era that the market became truly influential, by which stage the British government was issuing a variety of sovereign bonds including the earliest – the tontine – and the most popular, the consol, which is still in existence today. During the first half of the 19th century, Nathan Rothschild became one of the world's richest men, and arguably the most powerful banker in history, by effectively cornering the bond markets throughout Europe. His approval or otherwise of a country's debt came to have far-reaching consequences. Many historians now consider that France's ultimate defeat in the Napoleonic Wars owed more to its tendency to default on its debts, and its consequent difficulty in raising the necessary cash for its campaigns, than its strategic military decisions.

The yield curve Perhaps the most telling sign of the bond market's importance is the fact that the way bonds behave can provide excellent clues about the future of a particular economy. The yield curve simply measures the interest rates on a variety of different government bonds over time. All other things being equal, interest rates for bonds due to expire shortly should be lower than those which expire in a number of years – this reflects the fact that the economy is likely to grow in the future, and that inflation will rise. Occasionally, however, the yield curve becomes inverted, meaning that interest rates on bonds which expire soonest are higher than those expiring in future years.

This is a fairly reliable sign that the economy is heading for recession, since it implies interest rates and inflation will fall in the coming years – two phenomena usually associated with an economic slump. It is another example of how everyone's economic fate is inextricably tied into the state of the bond market.

the condensed idea
Bonds are the basis of government financing

28 Banks

Businesses, unlike people, are not created equal. There are some companies that would be missed if they ceased to exist, but life would go on. There are others whose collapse would cause vast sections of economies and societies to implode. Into this second category fall banks.

The companies that make up the banking and financial sector not only store our saved cash and lend us money when we need it, but act as the system of arteries that transports money around the economy, which is why they are often known as *financial intermediaries*. Their key function is to transfer money, en masse, from those who want to lend to those who want to borrow.

Banks have been a part of the social fabric of societies for centuries – indeed, the word 'bank' originates from the Latin word *banca*, which referred to the long desks that moneychangers in Ancient Rome would set up in courtyards to buy and sell foreign currency.

In order for an economy – whether rich or poor – to function properly, it must have a well-developed and healthy financial sector. Why? Because both companies and individuals invariably need to borrow to get started and subsequently to build decent, exciting, innovative businesses. Without banks, practically no one would be able to buy a house, since most people need to take out a mortgage in order to afford it.

Similarly, banks play an important role as a medium of exchange. Try to imagine living a day of your life without a bank. We use a bank card, credit card or cheque to pay for most of our shopping, banks thus being indirectly involved in almost every transaction we make.

timeline

5BC

Earliest examples of banking are seen in Ancient Greece

1397

Medici bank is founded – the world's first recognizable bank

At times, banks have grown into goliaths, and were recently found to be doing everything from running people's investments to owning industrial conglomerates and running hotels. Frequently, this level of power has generated resentment, people perceiving banks as parasitic – feeding off others' wealth in order to propagate their own. Occasionally these critics have had a point. As bank after bank crumbled in the late 2000s it became apparent that much of their expansion had not been based on fundamental growth. However, the plain truth is that without banks, people would not be able to borrow or invest – actions that are essential if they are to live productive, rewarding lives.

How do banks make their money? The basic structure and business model of a bank is fundamentally the same wherever you are in the world.

&What is robbing a bank compared with founding a bank?,

Bertolt Brecht

First, banks make a profit by charging more interest on the money they lend out than the money they have as deposits. The gap, or spread, between the two rates allows them to make some profit in return for providing this service, and the riskier a proposition you are (that is, the worse your credit rating), the wider the spread. This is why those taking out a mortgage worth more than 80 per cent or so of their prospective home are often charged a higher interest rate than others. They, after all, are more likely to default, forcing the bank to write off significant amounts of cash.

Second, banks offer customers other financial advice and services – often for a fee, sometimes merely to encourage them to deposit money with them. For individuals this might include insurance or investment advice. For businesses, it means helping them to issue stock and bonds (in other words to raise money, again connecting borrowers with lenders) and advising them on whether to take over other companies. This is the primary role of *investment banks*. They also use some of their surplus cash to invest themselves, hoping to make a little extra.

1800s	**1933**	**2007**
Rothschild family come to dominate European banking	The Federal Deposit Insurance Corporation is set up to protect savers' cash, originally with a $5,000 limit	A run on Northern Rock bank in the UK is followed by the collapse of Indymac in the US the following year

Banks' reserves

The key to modern finance is a system called fractional reserve banking. Say at any one point you have £1,000 left in your bank account. It's unlikely you'll need to take it all out at once. Although you might need your savings eventually, in reality you only withdraw fractions of them occasionally by visiting the bank counter, using an automatic teller machine (ATM) or bank card.

As a result, rather than leaving this cash sitting in their vaults, banks tend to keep only a fraction in their reserves, varying this amount depending on how much demand they expect for the money. Central banks typically control the amount of reserves banks are obliged to hold – in the US, for instance, the reserve requirement is usually 10 per cent, meaning a bank with a $100 deposit can lend out $90 worth of it.

This makes economic sense. It is far more efficient for banks to use the money deposited with them, maximizing its opportunity cost, rather than to leave it lying idle. However, there are important side-effects for the wider economy. By lending out this extra cash, banks will be adding to the money supply, and will push up inflation.

Bank runs The modern system of banking in which banks have less cash in their vaults than they officially owe their customers works fine when times are good and depositors are confident that their money is safe. However, in times of crisis, it can fail dramatically. If for some reason – rumours that a bank is about to collapse, for instance, or following a large robbery or natural disaster that affects the bank – large numbers of depositors may attempt to withdraw their money. This is called a bank run, and was spectacularly illustrated in the 2007 run on UK bank Northern Rock. When savers learnt that the bank had to receive emergency support from the Bank of England – in its role as lender of last resort – thousands of people swiftly queued to withdraw their money.

Because of fractional reserve banking, modern banks do not have enough ready cash to repay all their depositors at one time. As businesses, they are reliant on short-term borrowing (deposits) to fund long-term lending (mortgages and lengthy loans). The latter is highly illiquid, so if customers all demand back their money banks are left facing potential collapse. This would have been the case with Northern Rock had the UK Treasury not intervened and nationalized it.

❝A banker is a fellow who lends you his umbrella when the sun is shining and wants it back the minute it begins to rain.❞

Mark Twain

In the early days of banking, if a bank collapsed the savers faced losing all their money. This is what happened to many during the Great Depression. However, realizing this would cause public consternation and a run on deposits at the first sign of a bank being in trouble, governments have since set up deposit insurance schemes. In the US, the scheme is called the Federal Deposit Insurance Corporation, and in the UK the Financial Services Compensation Scheme; both protect deposits at banks to a certain amount (as of 2008, $250,000 and £50,000 respectively).

The experience of the financial crisis that started in 2008 has shown that governments will stop at almost nothing to ensure banks do not collapse. When they do, it can have dire consequences for the wider economy, not only denting consumer confidence and wealth, but also causing sharp falls in the money supply, as banks pour cash into their reserves and stop lending, which in turn can lead to deflation.

With their power to issue money, look after people's life savings, facilitate investment and provide the main arteries for spending, it is no wonder that banks are more regulated than just about any other type of business. Their health and that of the economy are inextricably linked.

the condensed idea
Banks connect borrowers with lenders

29 Stocks and shares

For as long as there has been money in the world there have been those who have wanted to invest it. In the earliest days of financial investment, from the Renaissance in Italy to the 17th century, the main outlet for such cash was government bonds, but everything changed with the birth of the world's first corporations. They ushered in a world of shares, of speculation, of millions made and millions lost and, of course, the earliest stock market crashes.

Every day investors buy and sell billions of dollars worth of shares on stock markets from London and Paris to New York and Tokyo. A company's share price can determine whether it will survive as an independent entity, whether it will be taken over, or whether, at the other extreme, it will go bust. Share prices can make people's fortunes and just as easily destroy them.

However, the stock market is no casino. The money people invest directly contributes towards the growth of a company and, by extension, the broader economy. A booming stock market is very often evidence of a thriving, fast-growing economy. This has been true since the first companies – or to give them their full title, joint-stock companies – were created to capitalize on the fast-expanding European colonial empires.

The original corporations Although the first recognizable company was the Virginia Company, set up to finance trade with colonists in America, the first major corporation was the British East India

timeline

1600	1792	1801
British East India Company founded	The Buttonwood Agreement lays the foundations for the establishment of the New York Stock Exchange	London Stock Exchange is founded

Company, which had a government-granted monopoly on trade with British territories in Asia. This was shortly followed by the Dutch East India Company in Amsterdam.

These first companies set themselves apart from their predecessors – guilds, partnerships and state-run enterprises – in the following ways:

1. *How they raised money.* The new companies issued shares or, as they are more often known today, equities. Unlike bonds, these give the shareholder formal ownership of a share in the company and, as such, much greater influence over its destiny. Shareholders can determine whether the company should buy or be sold to a rival through a merger or acquisition, and can vote on key issues, including directors' pay.
2. *Giving shareholders the right to sell their equities to other investors.* This created what is known as a secondary market, the stock market – as opposed to a primary market, in which the government or a company sells its bonds or shares directly to investors.
3. *Invoking so-called limited liability.* This means that if a company collapses its shareholders are only liable to lose what they have personally pumped into the business – not their house and car and all else besides. Companies also took on the legal guise of being a person in their own right – which gave corporations the right to sign contracts, own property and pay taxes themselves, independently of their shareholders.

As owners of the company, shareholders are entitled to a share in its profits. Provided the company is making surplus cash, after its running costs and investment plans are borne in mind, shareholders receive an annual *dividend* or payment. They can also profit when the value of the share increases, though they risk losing their investment if its value falls. If the company collapses, shareholders are further back in the

> **Most of the time common stocks are subject to irrational and excessive price fluctuations in both directions as the consequence of the ingrained tendency of most people to speculate or gamble . . .**
>
> **Benjamin Graham, US economist**

1929	**1987**
Wall Street Crash	Black Monday (19 October) – the US Stock market drops 22.6 per cent

Market movers and shakers

The creation of stock markets, where investors can buy and sell their equities, was one of the key turning points in the history of capitalism. Since then, the importance of shares has grown exponentially, and by late 2008 the total value of shares on world stock markets was around $37 trillion ($37,000,000,000,000). Every major economy around the world has a local stock market – usually in its capital city – on which the country's shares are traded.

The performance of these markets is generally measured by an index of the shares of their biggest companies. These are: the Dow Jones Industrials Average or the S&P 500 (the latter is a broader index) for New York; the FTSE 100 for London; the Nikkei for Tokyo; the DAX for Frankfurt; the CAC 40 for Euronext Paris; and the SSE Composite index for Shanghai.

queue to receive a payout than bondholders, so shares are generally regarded as riskier investments than debt.

In broad terms, companies can be divided into two types. There are those which are *private* or *unlisted*, whose shares are not on the open market. These are usually smaller companies, their shares typically owned solely by their directors and perhaps the family of the founder(s), banks and the original investors. Then there are those *listed publicly* – in other words, on stock markets.

The stock market The traditional image of a stock market is of a bustling, chaotic trading floor with aggressive traders shouting 'buy' and 'sell' at the top of their voices. In fact, there are very few so-called open-outcry markets left in the world – the main existing ones include the London Metals Exchange and the Chicago Mercantile Exchange. These trading floors have been replaced by computerized systems, allowing investors to trade directly from anywhere around the world.

Those who believe that the market is set to go up are known as *bulls* while those who expect a fall are referred to as *bears*. When investors become excited by the prospects of a particular company, they flock to buy its shares, which pushes the price higher. In contrast, if a company is struggling, investors will generally sell its stock and thus push the price lower.

En masse, investors are driven by a combination of fear and greed, and occasionally greed overpowers fear, causing a stock market bubble – where prices become overvalued – and sometimes fear overcomes greed, leading to the inevitable crash as shares come back down to earth with a bump. Stock markets in New York, London and elsewhere have suffered major bubbles in the last hundred years. Although the most notorious was the Wall Street Crash in 1929, share prices plummeted even more on Black Monday in 1987, when the Dow Jones dropped 22.6 per cent in a single day. Markets worldwide also suffered major falls following the dot-com crash between 2000 and 2002, and the financial crisis of 2008.

The big investors Participants in the stock market are split between *individual investors*, such as households with portfolios, and *institutional investors*, including pension funds, insurance groups, fund managers, banks and other institutions. Since pension and insurance funds own such a major stake in the stock market, changes in share prices indirectly affect almost every individual citizen.

Among the most maligned of the other investors are *hedge funds*, which not only buy shares but short sell them, meaning they make a bet on its value dropping. (The process of shorting stocks involves borrowing shares from another investor at a certain price, say $100, selling them on to the market at that price, waiting for the share to fall to, say $80, then buying it at the cheaper price, handing it back to the investor and pocketing the $20 difference.) Another type of investor is the *private equity firm*, which aims to buy up and overhaul struggling or undervalued businesses.

Many have come to see new investors such as private equity and hedge funds as a threat to the market, since they are highly secretive and are often seen to be blackmailing companies. They argue, however, that they have an invaluable market function by buying up undervalued or underperforming companies and overhauling them. After all, stock markets, where companies can be bought by members of the public, are inherently democratic institutions.

the condensed idea
Stock markets sit at the heart of capitalism

30 Risky business

'In this building it's either kill or be killed,' says Dan Ackroyd's character to Eddie Murphy in the 1983 movie *Trading Places*. They are striding into the futures and commodities market in New York, about to pull off the coup of the century. By first selling and then buying futures in frozen concentrated orange juice, the pair make millions for themselves and bankrupt their vindictive former employers.

For Barings, London's oldest merchant bank, it was 'be killed', with its collapse in 1995 after one of its traders, Nick Leeson, single-handedly lost millions of pounds on the futures market in Singapore.

Redistributing risk The futures and options markets – often known as derivatives markets – are perhaps the most risky and lucrative of all markets. And with good reason, for risk is precisely what the markets for commodities and financial derivatives deal in. This is where companies and traders speculate on what they expect to happen to prices of everything from stocks and shares, bonds and currencies, to metals and commodities, and even the weather and house prices.

Companies and individuals speculate not merely to gamble but for an essential economic purpose: to *redistribute risk*. They need to plan ahead in a highly unpredictable world. If you are a smoothie manufacturer, you do not know at the start of the year what sort of harvest to expect, and therefore how many oranges farmers will produce. Should the harvest be a disappointment, the price of oranges will rise sharply, but if the harvest is a bumper one, prices will fall because of the increase in the supply of oranges. You can choose to *hedge* your bets and secure a contract to buy

timeline

1730s	1800s
First recorded futures contracts are agreed on rice in the Dōjima Rice Exchange in Japan	The US sees a massive growth in agricultural contracts

orange juice at a given date in the summer for a fixed price. You cede your opportunity to make a saving if the harvest is good (or indeed to make a loss if it is bad) in return for the security of paying a certain sum. At the other end of the transaction, it also reduces the risk for the farmer, who is at least guaranteed some income that year.

The futures and options markets have become among the most important and busy in the world, as companies constantly have to make such judgements, whether it be a corn farmer fixing a price, or a big exporter such as Ford or Microsoft taking a position in currencies to ensure they do not lose out if the dollar suddenly falls.

Speculation and investment In order for the market to function there must be people willing to take on risk. This is where speculators come into the equation. While roughly half the participants in the futures markets are hedging, the rest are attempting to make money from betting on price movements. These pure speculators, who have their own suspicions about where the price will go, form an essential part of the economy. Sometimes they are individuals, sometimes hedge funds, sometimes pension funds looking to make a little more profit.

Either way, they are distinct from investors, who take a longer-term view. As Benjamin Graham, author of the seminal book for all investors, *The Intelligent Investor*, put it:

> The most realistic distinction between the investor and the speculator is found in their attitude toward stock-market movements. The speculator's primary interest lies in anticipating and profiting from market fluctuations. The investor's primary interest lies in acquiring and holding suitable securities at suitable prices.

It is possible to become rich by taking either path. The world's most famous investor is Warren Buffett, who tends to take long-term positions

1972	**1982**	**2008**
Futures trading on exchange rates is introduced in Chicago as currency markets become volatile	Equity futures trading is introduced	Total value of credit default swaps and other derivatives hits $1,144 trillion – 22 times the GDP of the entire world

Commodities, options and futures

Commodities constitute any type of solid material that can be bought or sold in bulk, from precious metals and oil to cocoa and coffee beans. If you want to buy it for instant delivery, you do so at the *spot price* – the instant price – as you would do with a share or a bond.

A *future* is a contract to buy a certain commodity or investment at a particular price at some point in the future (the delivery date).

An *option*, on the other hand, is an agreement that gives its holder the right, rather than the obligation, to buy or sell an investment at a particular price on a given day.

in companies and holds them, through his investment company Berkshire Hathaway, for years. In 2008 *Forbes* magazine valued him as the world's richest man with a fortune of $62 billion, though subsequently his wealth was significantly eroded by the effects of the financial crisis. The most famous hedge-fund billionaire is George Soros, who has made $9 billion by speculating on everything from share prices and commodities to currencies.

A brief history of futures A form of futures trading has existed for many centuries, deriving from the fact that there is often a gap between ordering a product and receiving it. In the 13th and 14th centuries, farmers often sold orders of wool a year or two in advance. In 18th-century Japan, merchants bought and sold rice for future delivery, and the first derivatives contracts were sold there to Samurai, who were usually paid in rice but, following a number of poor harvests, wanted to guarantee themselves a certain amount of income in the coming years.

However, it was in the 19th century that the market really took off – its spiritual home then and now being Chicago, where the futures market is called the Mercantile Exchange. For instance, in 1880 the Heinz food company signed contracts with farmers to buy cucumbers over future years at prearranged prices. Usually, however, a futures contract is not arranged directly between the buyer and seller, but via the futures exchange, which acts as a middleman. As expectations about the likely price of everything from pork bellies to metals to other commodities changes, so does the price of the futures associated with those commodities.

A zero-sum game This constant fluctuation is what makes the derivatives market such a risky place to invest. One has only to look at one of the biggest commodities and futures markets – that for crude oil – to see why. Oil prices rise and fall depending on a whole range of factors from economic (based, for instance, on the rate at which economies are likely to expand, and thus their likely demand for fuel) to geopolitical (based on the likelihood of terrorist attacks on oil platforms or relations between the Middle East and the rest of the world).

In 1999 the magazine *The Economist* predicted that, having dropped to $10 a barrel, oil prices would drop as low as $5. By the end of the year, its price was in fact up at $25. Between 2000 and 2005 it remained somewhere between $20 and $40 a barrel. Then, a combination of factors including the invasion of Iraq, red-hot economic growth in much of the world and fears about the amount of oil left in the ground, sent prices soaring, first to around $60, then to $80 and then, in 2008, all the way up to $140 a barrel. No sooner had it reached this level however, than it started to plummet, back down more or less to where it started as the global economy suffered recession.

By betting smartly on the price's direction of travel many investors made hundreds of millions of dollars, but just as many lost out. Unlike in the stock market, where shares in companies can all rise as they grow and flourish, futures contracts are zero-sum: for every winner there is someone who loses in similar magnitude. This is why the derivatives markets are often compared to a casino. But while a certain amount of gambling is involved, this is no idle pastime. These markets are an essential cog in the modern economic machine.

> **‘Be fearful when others are greedy and greedy only when others are fearful.’**
> **Warren Buffett**

the condensed idea
Pass risk to those more willing to take it

31 Boom and bust

Not that long after taking office as Chancellor of the Exchequer, Gordon Brown said in a number of speeches that he intended to free Britain from the old cycle of 'boom and bust'. It was music to everyone's ears. Britain had endured an unpleasant series of slumps, brought about by an overheating economy. Its citizens were ready to forgo a bit of boom if it meant not stomaching a bust.

Little more than a decade later and Brown, now Prime Minister, had stopped repeating the mantra. The economy was sliding towards a recession and its worst housing slump in living memory, if not ever. Most embarrassingly of all, the downturn was worse than that created by his political rivals, the Conservatives, when they had been in office. Leaving aside Brown's blushes, one thing was clear: reports of the business cycle's demise had been all too premature.

Economies by their very nature are prone to cycles of boom and bust: markets swing from confidence to pessimism and consumers from greed to fear. What controls these variables is not altogether understood because they are subject to the whims of human nature. And as Brown's experiences showed, attempts to tame the cycle have tended to fail dismally.

In theory, there ought to be an optimum level of economic activity at which a country could remain indefinitely. This is referred to as full employment; all the elements of production in an economy would be used to their optimum capacity. As such, inflation would not need to rise and the economy could grow at a consistent rate.

timeline

1929
Wall Street Crash

1946
Measuring Business Cycles
by Burns and Mitchell is published

In practice, however, this optimal point has never been reached. Cycles of various sorts have occurred throughout history. The Bible, for example, refers to periods of plenty succeeded by years of famine. The same rhythm applies to the sophisticated high-technology economies of the 21st century.

All major economies – the United States included – suffer these major swings in economic activity, which were first officially documented in 1946 by Arthur Burns and Wesley Mitchell.

The growth trend Every economy has a 'trend' growth rate – the speed at which the economy has tended to grow over recent decades. For the US in recent years this trend growth rate has been around 3 per cent, while in the UK and much of Europe it has been slightly lower at around 2.5 per cent, meaning that they have expanded at a slower rate. The business cycle (often called the economic cycle) is simply a fluctuation of economic activity above or below that growth rate. The difference between the two is known as the *output gap*. An economic cycle covers the time it takes for an economy to go through a boom, into a bust, and back to trend again.

> **The business cycle is doomed, thanks chiefly to the Government.**
>
> **Paul Samuelson, US economist**

At the peak, an economy can grow very fast indeed, but often this expansion is short-lived, giving way to a fall into negative territory – i.e. the economy contracts. If the economy contracts for two successive quarters it is technically in recession. This goes hand in hand with higher unemployment and falling profits among companies.

Why cycle? There are a number of explanations for cycles, though in truth none is as convincing as the fundamental fact that human beings are emotional creatures, and can swing very quickly from optimism to pessimism and vice versa. One explanation involves monetary policy: changes in interest rates, whether by private banks or central banks, have the knock-on effect of either speeding up or slowing down the economy's growth, as well as inflation and unemployment. Another technical

2007	2008
Beginning of the 2000s US economic bust, according to the National Bureau of Economic Research	Lehman Brothers collapses

Business cycles

Different parts of the economy ebb and flow from boom to bust in their own time and, from these, economists have devised a variety of classifications for cycles:

• **Kitchin cycle (3–5 years)** This refers to the rate at which businesses build up their inventories of goods, which in turn can make a country's economy speed up or slow down.

• **Juglar cycle (7–11 years)** This relates to how the amount companies spend on investment in their factories and services ebbs and flows – typically over roughly double the period of a Kitchin cycle. The Juglar cycle is what most economists are referring to when they talk about business cycles.

• **Kuznets cycle (15–25 years)** This is the length of time between booms in company or government spending on infrastructural investment, such as roads or railways.

• **Kondratiev wave or cycle (45–60 years)** Also known as a super-cycle, this refers more generally to phases of capitalism. The implication is that every 45 or 60 years there is a crisis of capitalism that leads people to question the way the economy is structured and the way it functions.

explanation revolves around the rate at which companies build up inventories – their hoards of unsold products. They tend to overstock these when growth is strong, since they expect the boom to continue, and to deplete them when the economy shrinks. In both cases, this makes the swings more violent than they ought to be.

Human experience is also an important factor. Some say that the seeds of a financial crisis are sown the year when the last banker who lived through the previous crisis retires. In other words, the more people forget the harsh consequences of a bust, the greater becomes the likelihood of similar mistakes being made again, generating another bubble.

In addition, unexpected events cause the economy to reel from one cycle to another. Clearly, few people expected the credit crisis that began in 2007 nor the collapse in oil prices a year later. The two together turned a downturn into a global recession. Perhaps the economy would behave more predictably without such shocks.

Others suspect that politicians are partly to blame, since they sometimes allow booms to get out of control in order to capitalize on the 'feel-good factor' generated by, for instance, soaring profits, rising house prices and high employment. They follow *pro-cyclical* policies – puffing air into the bubble – rather than *counter-cyclical* policies aimed at deflating bubbles gently before they explode.

Predicting the path The business cycle is clearly important. Having some idea of when an economy is about to stall is crucial, and governments employ teams of economists to attempt to diagnose this. In the US the chief experts are in the National Bureau of Economic Research, while in Britain they are found in the Treasury. Both have struggled in the past, often redefining their estimate of where a cycle begins and ends years (or even decades) after the event.

The problem is that cycles can vary dramatically in length (see box), so even if the starting-point is correctly identified, the estimate about when they will end may be well wide of the mark.

Many, including the world's most famous hedge-fund manager, George Soros, said that the crisis of the early 2000s was triggered by the end of a 'super-cycle' as people gradually built up more and more debt over decades. It would, he added, be followed by a similarly lengthy downturn, as people were forced to pay it all back.

The biggest frustration for economists is that economic cycles play havoc with the complex models they use to predict the economy's path. These computer models, into which they pour all the data they can find about jobs, prices, growth and so on, usually assume that the economy will carry on in a more or less straight line forever. Experience, however, shows that this is simply not the case.

the condensed idea
Boom and bust are inevitable

32 Pensions and the welfare state

The year is 1861 and the Civil War is tearing America apart. As both the Unionists and the Confederates struggle to attract fresh recruits to their armies, someone comes up with an ingenious plan: offer generous pensions to soldiers and their widows. It seems to do the trick – hundreds of thousands swiftly join the fight.

When do you suppose the last payment was made from the Civil War pension scheme? The 1930s or 1940s, when the oldest war veterans were approaching the end of their lives? In fact, the scheme did not make its final payout until 2004. One enterprising 21-year-old woman had taken it upon herself to marry an 81-year-old veteran in the 1920s, leaving the state with a remarkably long-lasting bill until she died at the age of 97.

Imagine this same problem writ large across not just a whole nation, but the entire developed world, governments having promised to provide generously for their elderly citizens, only to realize decades later that the same citizens are living too long and sucking up too much of their cash. Behold the pensions and welfare crisis.

Evolution of the welfare state Although states have occasionally offered pensions, education and other benefits to some of their citizens since Roman times – usually in exchange for military service – the existence throughout the world of welfare states and social security systems is a relatively new phenomenon. Until the 20th century countries tended to tax their citizens purely in order to protect them from crime and

timeline

1880

Bismarck sets up the first state pension and medical insurance scheme invasion. However, in the wake of the First World War and the Great Depression, as the scale of penury faced by so many families became clear, countries such as the UK and US evolved into 'welfare states' – where taxes are used to redistribute money to those judged most in need – whether it be the old, infirm, unemployed or sick. The original model was developed in Germany by Bismarck only a decade or so after the Civil War ended on the other side of the Atlantic.

The theory behind pensions and social security is as simple today as when the system was first devised: the citizens of a country should contribute towards a general fund when they are in work and good health, and in return that fund will help provide for their welfare when they are sick, unable to work or want to retire.

The Beveridge Report

The catalyst in the creation of welfare states was William Beveridge's seminal 1942 *Report of the Inter-departmental Committee on Social Insurance and Allied Services*, designed to clamp down on 'Want, Disease, Ignorance, Squalor and Idleness'. As governments turned half an eye to the post-war world, it became clear that something needed to be done to ensure that people were properly supported in the future, and the Beveridge Report provided an ideal template. The combined ordeal of the Great Depression and the war had highlighted the fact that, in certain extreme circumstances, the private sector simply could not protect people from hardship. However, the report argued that, given the state's size and hence bargaining potential, it could secure better, cheaper and more economical healthcare and pensions for its citizens.

Nowhere were Beveridge's ideas more enthusiastically applied than in Japan, which dramatically improved its citizens' life expectancy and educational qualifications by setting up a major system of social security, hospitals and schools after the war. The quality of its giant welfare state is widely regarded as having helped the country bounce back so vigorously in subsequent years.

1908

David Lloyd George introduces pensions in the UK

1942

The Beveridge Report is published

The problems Despite it having pulled many families out of poverty, and having dramatically improved health and academic standards throughout the Western world, many argue that the welfare state has also brought with it some major problems: one socio-economic, the other fiscal.

The socio-economic quandary is that state welfare systems can discourage people from working. There is much evidence to suggest that offering unemployed workers income support can discourage them from going out and looking for another job (see chapter 22). Despite having swelled to mammoth proportions, welfare spending appears over recent decades actually to have reduced productivity in various countries, including the UK and various northern European states.

> 'Pension reforms, like investment advice and automatic enrolment, will strengthen the ability of Americans to save and invest for retirement.'
>
> Steve Bartlett, former US congressman

Then there is the problem of how to fund such systems in the long run. Most social welfare systems are funded out of governments' current budgets: they are largely pay-as-you-go, with today's taxpayers funding the pensions bills for today's retirees rather than their own future pensions. Such a system worked very successfully in the post-war years: the massive explosion of population in the late 1940s and 1950s – the so-called 'baby boom' – meant there were plenty of young workers paying their taxes into the pot throughout the 1960s, 1970s and 1980s. However, with fertility having dwindled since, various countries, including the US, UK, Japan and much of Europe, are facing a massive bill in the future.

The problem is particularly acute in the US. The American system includes a state pension for all ('social security'), Medicare – free health insurance for the elderly – and a number of other smaller programmes including Medicaid – health cover for the poor – and temporary unemployment support. However, the system is facing a major crunch as the baby-boomer generation retires. The share of the US population aged 65 or over is set to increase from 12 per cent to nearly 21 per cent by 2050, with this crop of pensioners living longer and demanding more medical care than ever before.

Welfare in the future According to generational economists, who study the way one generation's decisions can impinge on the next, the

Solutions to the pensions and welfare crisis

1. Allow more immigrants to come and work in the country. This would increase the size of the workforce – plus many of them would retire to their own countries without claiming the state pension.
2. Raise taxes on future taxpayers to help pay the bill but, as a consequence, accept weaker economic growth.
3. Force pensioners either to work longer or to accept lower payments.
4. Throw out the existing pay-as-you-go welfare systems in favour of programmes in which taxpayers have to contribute a certain amount into a fund each month. Already a number of governments are moving in this direction – including the UK. However, the reforms are likely to arrive too late to prevent an uncomfortable squeeze on public finances in the coming years.

costs of welfare in the coming years – tied to the shrinking size of the working population – means that the US is, by most definitions of the term, heading for outright bankruptcy. Similar predictions could be made of Japan, where over 21 per cent of the population is already over 65, projected to rise to equal the working population by 2044.

There is evidence that fertility rates have started to increase slightly in the UK and US, thanks largely to a glut of teenage pregnancies in the former and the fecundity of Mexican immigrants in the latter. However, even this is unlikely to spare either country from an impending shock.

The painful truth is that either the pensioners will have to accept less generous handouts or tomorrow's citizens will have to pay more in taxes. It is a quandary that will dominate politics and economics for some decades to come.

the condensed idea
Beware promising money you can't give

33 Money markets

In an unremarkable office block somewhere in London's Docklands a small band of people are charged with producing perhaps the world's most important number. The level of that number, fixed at 11 o'clock each morning, will have far-reaching consequences throughout the world: it will send some into bankruptcy, make others millions. It is a part of the very foundations of capitalism. And yet very few people outside the financial markets even know about it. It is the London Interbank Offered Rate (Libor).

The Libor rate, which is administered by the British Bankers Association, sits at the hub of one of the key sectors of the world economy – the money markets. It is here that companies borrow and lend money in the short term – in other words, without having to issue bonds or equities (see chapter 27). These markets are the central nervous system of the world's financial system, and when, occasionally, they fail, it can send the entire economy into shock.

In normal times, Libor simply reflects the rate at which banks are willing to lend to each other in the short term. This lending – often referred to as *interbank lending* – is unsecured: it is rather like an overdraft or credit card as opposed to a mortgage, and is essential for banks to function. Every day, a bank's balance sheet changes significantly as people deposit, withdraw, borrow and repay cash, and so being able to borrow from one another at short notice is essential for banks to stay afloat.

The way in which banks operate has undergone various transformations over the past decades. Traditionally, banks would make their money by

timeline

1970s	1984
Securitization first developed	The British Bankers' Association sets up Libor

The power of Libor

So powerful and expansive have the wholesale money markets become that the London Interbank Offered Rates – which are broken down into the world's major currencies including the dollar, euro and sterling – are at the heart of contracts worth around $300 trillion – equivalent to $45,000 for each human being on the planet. Most people think of interest rates as the official rate laid down by central banks such as the Federal Reserve or Bank of England. In fact, Libor is a far better indication of the real cost of borrowing in the broader economy.

taking in customers' deposits in the form of savings and lending out this cash to other customers as mortgages and other types of loan (see chapter 28). On the one hand this meant that, rather as George Bailey (played by James Stewart) attempts to pacify depositors who are frantically withdrawing cash in *It's a Wonderful Life*, the banks had a direct connection – often a personal relationship – with their customers. On the other hand, this *modus operandi* didn't provide the banks with as many opportunities for growth as they wanted because there were rules laid down by regulators about how much they were allowed to lend in comparison with their size. This, in turn, meant they weren't as likely to charge low mortgage rates.

Rise of securitization Many of these banks, or mortgage lenders, were set up as mutual associations, meaning they were owned not by shareholders but by their customers. In the UK, such specialized mortgage lenders were known as building societies, and included companies such as Nationwide and Northern Rock.

However, in the 1970s and 1980s, as demand for home ownership grew (see chapter 37) and banks realized it would be difficult to keep up without boosting the amount of cash they had available to lend, they turned to an

1980s–90s

Banks around the world
expand rapidly

2007

Interbank markets freeze up

alternative system. Rather than lending cash based solely on their deposits, they started to bundle up the mortgage debt they were issuing into packages and selling it on to other investors. The process was known as *securitization* – because it turned debt into securities (investment instruments such as bonds, options, shares, etc.) – and worked very well for a time. By taking the mortgage debt off their books, the banks were able to lend out more and bigger mortgages without being limited by their size. Investors from around the world queued up to buy the securities, lured by the healthy return the securities paid and the reassurance of credit ratings agencies that they were reliable investments.

Over time, banks have become increasingly sophisticated in how they create these securities. Not only have they bundled mortgages together into packages; they have also sliced and diced them into instruments known as collateralized debt obligations (CDOs), and even more complex versions such as $CDOs^2$ (effectively sliced and diced twice) and $CDOs^3$ (cubed).

The theory behind such activities seems quite sensible. Previously, if a mortgage holder defaulted on his debts, the main party to suffer would be the bank; securitization promised to spread that risk around the financial system to those more willing to take it on. The problem, however, is that by eliminating the personal relationship between borrower and lender (a process called *disintermediation*), there is a far greater likelihood that whoever ends up buying the package of debts – whether they are Japanese investors or European pension funds – will not appreciate the true picture of the risks they are taking on. All they have to rely on are the ratings handed down by agencies such as Standard & Poors, Fitch and Moody's, and so on.

This disconnection was one of the main causes of the financial crisis of the 2000s, since investors were not fully aware of the scale of risk they were taking on when they bought such immensely complicated bundles of debt. Since banks were lending out far more than they had in deposits, they developed a major shortfall in their accounts – a hole widely known as the *funding gap* – which can only be filled by wholesale funding. As we will see, this was not forthcoming.

The day that changed the world On 9 August 2007, both interbank markets and markets for securitized mortgages seized up suddenly all around the world. Realizing that the US housing market was facing a major slide, and that, more fundamentally, the Western financial system had become excessively indebted, investors stopped buying securities – in other words, they stopped lending money. It was a moment of fear that triggered the financial crisis to follow; the moment when economists and financiers, who had until then paid this complex part of the system scant attention, realized its importance to the health of the world economy.

Many banks on both sides of the Atlantic, including Northern Rock, were suddenly unable to fund themselves from the wholesale markets. They were left with a massive black hole in their accounts. Although the financial crisis had many causes, it was this freeze in the financial markets that sent the first fatal shocks through the system. Barely a month later Northern Rock was forced to seek emergency funding from the Bank of England, which acted as a lender of last resort. Although many assume that the problem was caused specifically by subprime mortgages (i.e. home loans made to people of low creditworthiness), the real issue for Northern Rock was that it was so entirely reliant on the wholesale markets, where Libor rates had shot up, reflecting banks' reluctance to lend to each other.

> **❛I don't think that any economist disputes that we're in the worst economic crisis since the Great Depression. The good news is that we're getting a consensus around what needs to be done.❜**
>
> **Barack Obama**

The Libor rate is only an indicative rate, showing what banks would in theory be willing to charge each other. In this case, there was no lending occurring whatsoever. Central banks were forced to step in and pump money directly into markets and banks themselves. The money markets had dried up!

the condensed idea
Money markets make the financial world go round

34 Blowing bubbles

Irrational exuberance: two rather unremarkable words, but when put together they had enough force to cause stock markets around the world to plunge. When in 1996 Alan Greenspan, then Chairman of the Federal Reserve, warned that this was what markets could be experiencing, it caused a major slide in prices as investors questioned whether they were trapped inside a bubble.

Greenspan had realized that the share prices of technology firms were rising far faster than one might have expected. People were getting carried away, allowing their excitement about the Internet boom to push them into buying shares for more than they were reasonably worth. The result, in the early days of the dot-com share bubble, had been to send prices soaring. Greenspan's warning caused the Dow Jones share index in Wall Street to dip by 145 points the following day, but confidence recovered until after the turn of the millennium.

This 'irrational exuberance' affair illustrates two key points about financial markets and bubbles: first, it is extremely difficult to identify a bubble, still more so to work out how close it is to popping; second, it is not always easy to bring bubbles back under control.

Identifying bubbles Economic bubbles occur when speculators' and investors' excitement about a particular asset causes its price to be pushed higher than it ought to be. Of course, gauging the 'right' price is subjective,

timeline

1637	1720	1840
Tulip bubble in the Netherlands	South Sea bubble, Mississippi Company bubble	Mania in railway investment

> **‘Our [investment decisions] can only be taken as the result of animal spirits – a spontaneous urge to action rather than inaction.’**
> **John Maynard Keynes**

hence the problem. Even as Internet share prices scaled dizzy heights in 2000 there were plenty of analysts and experts who maintained they were fairly valued. The same was true of house prices in the US and the UK in 2006 before they started to slump during the following economic crisis.

Bubbles are by no means a new phenomenon. They have recurred since the earliest days of markets: from 17th-century Holland, where investors rushed into buying tulips, and the South Sea and Mississippi Company bubbles of the 18th century (associated with profits to be made from European colonies), through to the various property crazes of the 20th century.

While it is obvious with hindsight that these were bubbles, it was hard to identify them in advance. Prices can rise for what economists call 'fundamental' reasons. House prices, for example, may increase because more people want to live in a certain country or region – in other words, there's an increase in demand – or because the number of homes being built falls – in other words, there's a constraint on supply.

Leaning against the wind Many economic experts, including Alan Greenspan, have argued that policymakers should not attempt to clamp down on bubbles – to 'lean against the wind' by, most obviously, raising interest rates or slapping down new regulations – but should instead concentrate on mopping up the mess after they burst. Their rationale is

1926	**1989**	**2001**	**2006–8**
Florida property crash	UK property bubble bursts	Dot-com bubble pops	Property bubbles pop in the US, UK and much of the Western world

Feedback loops

When a bubble is brewing or bursting, it affects the economy through a virtuous or vicious cycle, which economists call a positive or negative feedback loop. As prices rise, people feel wealthier, causing them to spend more, which propels the wider economy forward. When prices slump, people spend less, which in turn causes prices to fall even further and banks to lend less cash. During the 2008 financial crisis, a negative feedback loop developed, in which banks stopped lending freely to the public, which prompted people to cut back on their spending, which only served to reinforce banks' reluctance to lend. These loops are the most dangerous of all economic phenomena, since once started they are very difficult for anyone – from central banks to politicians – to arrest.

twofold. First, it is difficult to identify whether rising prices are the symptom of a bubble or a benign manifestation of economic growth. Second, given that economic tools such as interest rates and regulation are blunt, the likelihood is that employing them will lead to collateral damage in other parts of the economy.

Some have actually suggested that bubbles are an integral part of a well-functioning economy, encouraging large-scale investment that would not otherwise have occurred. For instance, the dot-com boom of the late 1990s sparked a race to lay massive fibre-optic links across the world. The result was an international network of far greater capacity than was needed at the time. Many of the firms involved went bust, but the increase in bandwidth was partly responsible for driving economic growth in the post dot-com years, as it brought down the price of international communication. Similarly, some argue that the popping of a bubble rids the economy of its least successful businesses through the process of creative destruction (see chapter 36).

The damage done However, such arguments can seem questionable when an economy has just suffered the bursting of a bubble. The slump or recession that follows can be highly damaging. As banks start rationing credit, for example, even simple financial transactions can become significantly more expensive (see chapter 35). One has only to look at the Great Depression, which followed on from the Wall Street Crash of 1929, to realize how serious the long-term economic implications of a bursting bubble can be.

Some maintain that economic bubbles distract people with the lure of easy money from what they ought to be investing in. In economic terms, they cause a misallocation of resources that would be better used elsewhere. For example, investors may buy up houses in the belief that the price will appreciate, rather than spend the money on shares or putting it into savings.

Dulling the cycle There are various ways in which those running an economy can prevent bubbles from developing. The first tool of choice is simply to signal – through a speech or some other public announcement – that policymakers are concerned about a bubble developing (possibly indicating also that measures will be taken to prevent it). However, as the dot-com crash showed, this is not guaranteed to prevent the bubble from ballooning. The second option is to raise interest rates, which can dampen the growth of the bubble but at the cost of slowing growth in other parts of the economy. A third idea is to regulate banks more tightly to ensure they do not lend out cash too freely when times are good, and then, in the wake of a burst bubble, simply shut up shop. Such policies are known as *counter-cyclical* since they aim to prevent the economy swinging from boom into bust – as opposed to *pro-cyclical* policies, which encourage bubbles and then painful slumps.

In the wake of the 2008 crisis, central banks pledged to do more to 'lean against the wind' and prevent house-price bubbles from emerging again – as had happened so disastrously during that decade. However, economists have become increasingly convinced that bubbles remain an unavoidable part of economic growth. For as long as humans remain irrational and unpredictable, bubbles are likely to be a permanent part of life.

**the condensed idea
Humans are addicted
to bubbles**

35 Credit crunches

$$C = SN(d_1) - Le^{-rT} N(d_1 - \sigma \sqrt{T})$$

It may not look like much, but it is the most dangerous equation since $E=mc^2$. Just as Albert Einstein's equation led eventually to Hiroshima and Nagasaki, this one has had the financial impact of a nuclear bomb. It contributed to stock market booms and busts, to a succession of financial crises, and to economic slumps that lost millions of people massive chunks of their livelihood. It is the Black-Scholes formula, and at the heart of its story is the biggest economic question of all: can humans learn from their mistakes?

There are, broadly speaking, two schools of thought over the way financial markets behave. One is that human beings tend to lurch from a state of fear to one of greed, and that markets can become obsessive and essentially irrational at the extreme. Its conclusion is that we will always go from one bubble to another. This is the theory of credit cycles. When times are good, money is cheap and abundant, but occasionally such times are interrupted by a credit crunch – where banks simply stop lending, causing normal economic life virtually to grind to a halt.

The other theory is that, over time, markets are self-correcting, gradually becoming more efficient and less prone to neuroses, which means that crashes and crunches will eventually become a thing of the past. The theory hinges on the belief that humans, in the long run, can improve themselves. It is to this thesis that the wonder equation, devised by Myron Scholes and Fischer Black, was devoted.

timeline

1873
Panic caused by the post-Civil War bubble triggers the Long Depression in the US

1929
Wall Street Crash triggers a liquidity crisis and the Great Depression

Black swans

A 'black swan' is shorthand for an unexpected event that forces people to revise their preconceived views of the world. The term, popularized by the writer and former trader Nassim Nicholas Taleb, derives from the assumption in pre-17th-century Europe that all swans were white; a notion disproved by the discovery of black swans in Australia.

In financial markets, a black-swan event is a random, unexpected moment that causes markets either to plunge or to soar. Taleb describes the arrival of the Internet as one moment, and the Russian government's decision to default on its debt in 1998 as another. The former led to the dot-com boom, the latter to a major debt crisis and the collapse of Long-Term Capital Management, one of the world's biggest hedge funds. Another example is the September 11 attacks in 2001.

The Black-Scholes equation did the seemingly impossible. On the face of it, it was merely a means of working out how an option on derivatives markets (see chapter 30) should be priced. However, the implications were staggering. It was a mathematical formula that apparently took the risk out of investing in the markets. By following the equation, it seemed, investors could avoid losing millions merely by selling stocks short (in other words, betting on their imminent decline) when prices were plunging. The formula was adopted by almost every major investor around the world and won its creators the Nobel Prize for Economics in 1997. Unfortunately though, when the going got tough, it didn't work. In a situation where prices were falling so fast that there were no buyers for a particular stock, share or investment, the highly logical equation broke down.

The problem for the equation – as indeed for just about all economic theories – is that since the dawn of time markets have behaved irrationally. Booms and busts seem to be an inevitable component of market capitalism (see chapter 31).

1987

Black Monday (19 October) – US stock market crashes 22.6 per cent

2008

Markets around the world slump after the financial crisis claims investment bank Lehman Brothers

The stages from boom to bust Financial markets are absolutely integral to the health of economies, since without easy access to credit (or to give it its other name, debt), businesses and individuals cannot invest for their futures. When money available for borrowing is in short supply, the resulting credit crunch can lead to recession or, even worse, deflation and depression, as people stop investing and creating wealth. So understanding how a financial market lurches from greed to fear is central to understanding how a modern economy functions.

Financial markets go through five stages from boom to bust. They are as follows:

6As long as the music is playing, you've got to get up and dance. We're still dancing.9

Chuck Prince, chief executive of Citigroup until 2007

1. *Displacement.* Something happens to change investors' perceptions about the markets. In the late 1990s it was the Internet, which – until the dot-com crash – people believed offered almost limitless money-making potential. In the early 2000s it was a combination of low interest rates and low inflation, which persuaded people to take out more debt, as well as to invest in housing.

2. *Boom.* Investors' hopes about the benefits of this displacement (often called a 'new paradigm') seem to pay off. In the 1990s, for example, those who bought Internet stocks saw their investments leap in price, while house prices soared in the early 2000s, thanks to low interest rates and the belief that banks had discovered a new, risk-free model of mortgage funding.

3. *Euphoria.* Excitement takes hold and banks lend ever more money in a bid to increase profits. Often they invent new financial instruments to facilitate this. In the 1980s, the innovation was junk bonds – bonds of dubious quality; in the early 2000s it was the securitization of mortgages and other debts. Everyone – from the steady investor to the taxi driver – dives into the market.

4. *Profit-taking.* Smart investors suddenly realize the good times cannot go on forever, so start selling off their investments. As they sell, prices start falling for the first time.

5. *Panic.* With prices now falling, fear spreads. People rush to sell their investments en masse, and prices plunge sharply. Banks stop lending to any but the most creditworthy.

> ❛**The market can stay irrational longer than you can stay solvent.**❜
> **John Maynard Keynes**

The five stages, laid out by economist Hyman Minsky, have repeated themselves throughout history, although each time the original displacement and precise details of the boom differed. In a sense, history does repeat itself, but each time it is so camouflaged as to be almost unrecognizable. The problem is that when a market panics, the result is often a liquidity crisis.

The Minsky moment During the panic stage, prices can fall so far and so fast that the value of the assets in question – for instance, housing – swiftly drops below the amount of debt people have taken out to buy them in the first place. Banks start calling in their loans, but because it is hard to sell a speculative asset, investors sell them at a lower price, or find something else to sell. Either way, the result is that prices fall even further. This vicious circle is sometimes known as a 'Minsky moment'.

Such behaviour – panic and mania – seems irrational, and because conventional economics makes very little allowance for irrational behaviour, it has often been slow to diagnose impending bubbles and crashes before it is too late. The Black-Scholes equation was grounded in the idea that there will always be demand for a particular share or investment, provided the price comes down to an attractive level, but failed to account for irrational behaviour during a crisis. As with so many sophisticated models and equations, it reinforced the delusion that we can somehow escape from risk. But the financial world has always been a risky place.

the condensed idea
Economies seize up as credit dries up

36 Creative destruction

It is widely known that Charles Darwin's theory of evolution was of groundbreaking scientific importance, ranking alongside Isaac Newton's discovery of gravity and the laws of motion, or Copernicus's realization that the earth revolves around the sun. Few realize, however, that Darwin may never have come to his epiphany were it not for economics.

In 1838, Darwin was inspired by writings of Thomas Malthus (see chapter 3) to imagine a world in which the fittest survive and can evolve into new, more sophisticated and better-equipped species. 'I had at last,' he said, 'got a theory by which to work.' And when you look at them, the forces that shape both the natural world and free-market economics are uncannily similar.

Law of the economic jungle Like nature, free markets can be nasty. They sometimes cause talented and worthy individuals to fail. They are unforgiving: if an idea of yours does not succeed it can mean bankruptcy; if you make a bad investment you could stand to lose everything. However, according to the law of creative destruction, such failures can ultimately serve to make stronger companies, stronger economies and wealthier societies because they weed out the old, inefficient and most uncompetitive to make way for the new, the vibrant and the strong.

It is an extension of the rules of supply and demand laid down by Adam Smith, but the law of creative destruction, devised by a group of Austrian economists in the 20th century, takes it one step further. It claims that a

timeline

1883

Joseph Schumpeter born

recession or an economic downturn, in which unemployment rises as firms face falling profits, could, counter-intuitively, be positive for an economy in the long run.

Such a claim was made most vigorously by Joseph Schumpeter, an Austrian who emigrated to the United States to escape Nazi persecution. His contention that recessions should not be avoided was as controversial then as it is now. The doctrine supported by most economists at the time (and most politicians even now) was that policymakers should do whatever possible to avoid recessions and, in particular, depressions. John Maynard Keynes notably argued that these cause such significant collateral damage, in terms of unemployment and slumping confidence, that they should be countered by every means at a government's disposal, such as cutting interest rates and spending public funds to kick-start the economy.

Most economists typically rely on complex computer models that assume competition is perfect and supply and demand remain more or less static over time. Schumpeter claimed that such models bear little resemblance to the volatile conditions in which societies are forged.

Schumpeter's argument, far from being quashed, has retained its strength. In fact, according to prominent economists Brad DeLong and Larry Summers, just as Keynes was the most important economist of the 20th century, Schumpeter may well prove to be the most important of the 21st.

❛The process of industrial mutation . . . incessantly revolutionizes the economic structure from within, incessantly destroying the old one, incessantly creating a new one . . . This process of Creative Destruction is the essential fact about capitalism.❜

Joseph Schumpeter

1930s

Great Depression causes hundreds of thousands of business failures

1942

Schumpeter popularizes the idea of creative destruction in his book *Capitalism, Socialism and Democracy*

JOSEPH SCHUMPETER 1883–1950

Schumpeter hailed originally from what is now the Czech Republic, but moved to Vienna, Austria, when his mother remarried. There, his aristocratic stepfather helped him gain entrance to elite colleges, where he soon stood out as a brilliant student. Indeed, not long afterwards he embarked on a remarkably illustrious career: first as professor of economics and government at a number of universities, and then, after the First World War, as Austrian Minister of Finance, finally becoming president of Biederman Bank in 1920. However, the bank collapsed in 1924, leaving Schumpeter bankrupt and forcing him back into academia. With the rise of Nazism in the 1930s he moved to America, where he was fast recognized as a top intellectual. He spent the rest of his career at Harvard, gaining something of a cult following among students and professors alike. He was, by the 1940s, one of America's most renowned economists, becoming president of the American Economic Association in 1948.

Rebirth through recession Rather than rolling along at a constant rate, economies are prone to so-called cycles of boom and bust (see chapter 31). During a boom, when consumers are spending more than usual and often borrowing more, it is comparatively easy for businesses to make money. Schumpeter argued that this leads to inefficient firms that, in less favourable times, would not even have been formed in the first place.

Conversely, when the economy slumps and people spend less, inefficient companies go bankrupt. While this causes pain in the short term, it also forces investors to put their money into other, more attractive parts of the economy. This in turn boosts the potential growth rate for the economy in the years ahead. Schumpeter and his fellow Austrian, Friedrich Hayek (see chapter 12), thus argued that governments should not slash interest rates massively to prevent recessions. Instead, they argued, those who made unprofitable investments during booms should suffer the consequences, or else the same mistakes would invariably be made in the future.

Such logic applies to entire industries as much as individual firms. For example, lean times in recent years, brought about by competition from overseas, have forced manufacturing industry in the United States and Europe to contract and become more streamlined, inefficient firms having been weeded out.

Survival of the fittest The theory was put into practice during the Great Depression of the 1930s, when US policymakers allowed thousands of banks to collapse, hoping for a cathartic recovery. US Treasury Secretary at the time, Andrew Mellon, urged investors to 'liquidate labour, liquidate stocks, liquidate the farmers, and liquidate real estate . . . It will purge the rottenness out of the system.' In the following years, the economy lost a third of its wealth and took decades to fully recover. That hardly seems like a creative type of destruction and, unsurprisingly, the idea subsequently fell out of favour. Recent studies showing that firms are often more likely to restructure and streamline during boom times rather than in busts have reinforced scepticism.

Schumpeter and Hayek, however, argued that there is an important difference between a shallow downturn and a full-blown depression, which lasts for years and causes irreparable damage. In addition, for the creative destruction rule to work, economies must be flexible enough to cope with the ebbs and flows caused by downturns. In many European economies where labour markets are strictly regulated and it is difficult for firms to hire and fire, it may be harder than it ought to be for those who have lost their jobs in a downturn to find employment again. In such cases, recessions can have a permanent cost that outweighs the longer-term benefits promised by creative destruction.

> ‘**Economic progress, in capitalist society, means turmoil.**’
>
> **Joseph Schumpeter**

The lasting message is that out of the ashes of an economic slump can come a stronger and healthier economy. Of the top 100 global companies in 1912, only 19 remained in the list by 1995, with nearly half having disappeared, collapsed or been taken over. However, it is precisely because of creative destruction that the economy has grown so successfully in that period. Research shows that most recessions in American history have tended to improve productivity rather than dampening it. So, just as evolution over time leaves species better equipped to adapt to their environment, creative destruction has created better functioning economies.

the condensed idea
Companies must adapt or die

37 Home-owning and house prices

For most of us our home is our greatest asset and most valuable possession. In order to purchase a house, we have to borrow more than we ever would in other circumstances, taking out a loan that lasts for a generation. And if we are unlucky enough to buy it at the wrong moment, there is every chance it could ruin us.

Since the earliest years of the 20th century, home-buying has been a major obsession among those who live in rich economies. Home ownership has risen from below one-quarter of the population to almost three-quarters in many parts of the Western world. However, it was this push for broader owner-occupation that helped trigger the financial crisis of the late 2000s, and the idea of universal home ownership has now come under major scrutiny.

No ordinary asset In pure economic terms, property is regarded merely as a type of asset. It is relatively easily to buy and sell and has a value that tends either to rise or fall as time passes. However, unlike most other assets – such as shares, wine, paintings or gold coins – property also serves an essential function: it is a place in which to live.

The conjunction between these two factors means that a house-price boom – followed by its subsequent bust – has far more wide-ranging effects than does a stock market slump or a fall in other asset prices.

timeline

1920s–30s	1989
UK sees a massive jump in home-building, followed by a slump	UK suffers a major housing crash, lasting more than half a decade and wiping a third off real house prices

When house prices are booming it contributes to a rise in consumer confidence across an entire economy. People typically spend and borrow more, since they know the value of their home has increased. This is not only a matter of confidence: home-owners can also borrow against the increased value of their property through what is known as *mortgage equity withdrawal*.

On the flip-side, when house prices fall sharply it has extremely damaging social effects that could hardly be mirrored by a plunge in any other type of asset. When a family's house falls so far in value that it becomes worth less than the mortgage, then that family is trapped in *negative equity*. This is not a major issue (though confidence-sapping nevertheless) unless the home-owner needs to sell. In order to do that they would have either to trade down or to pay their mortgage company the difference.

Bubbles and busts It was always felt there are few more reliable investments than housing, and there is some truth in that. Since 1975, house prices in the United Kingdom increased at an average annual real rate (i.e. taking away inflation) of just under 3 per cent. But the behaviour of house prices is dependent on a number of factors. First, there is the cost of the land that the house sits on. If the demand for land increases (or the supply of available land or homes constricts) this pushes up house prices. Likewise, if the supply of housing suddenly increases, prices will fall. One of the factors behind the massive drop in house prices in Miami in 2008 was the completion of a glut of new housing developments that crowded out other sales.

> **❝You'd have to be either mad or a publicity seeker to predict what is going to happen to house prices.❞**
>
> **Mervyn King, Governor of Bank of England**

Professor Robert Schiller, an economics professor at Yale and a leading housing expert, also points out that prices tend to boom more in areas where there are greater restrictions on planning and building. So in California and Florida – where there are more stringent planning

early 2000s	2007	2008
Home ownership in both the US and UK hits record levels of around 70 per cent as more families buy homes	House prices in the US fall nationwide for the first time on record	Housing markets in the US, UK, Australia, New Zealand, Ireland and elsewhere are embroiled in housing slumps

restrictions – prices soared and then collapsed, whereas in Houston, Texas – where there are few restrictions – they barely budged off their long-term price increase.

That long-term increase is usually similar to the long-term growth rate of an economy. This makes sense. In the long run one would expect house prices to increase at about the same rate as an economy's overall wealth grows.

However the fact is that house prices have been prone to a number of major booms and busts in the past 50 years, culminating in 2008 in house-price falls in both the US and UK the speed of which had not been seen since the Great Depression. Why are house prices so prone to such jolts?

The increase in home ownership The main underlying reason for house-price volatility is that in both the US and UK, successive governments have made it their stated aim to increase levels of home ownership as much as is humanly possible. To see the effect of this one only has to look at the UK. There, until the First World War, a mere tenth of homes were owned by their occupier, compared with almost half in the US. This was partly because much of the property was owned by the richest members of the population and rented out, but it was also partly a social phenomenon. Even the wealthiest young men would prefer to take rooms – lodgings – rather than buy or rent their own properties when coming to London. In most circles it was perfectly normal never to own your own house.

> **❝I made a tremendous amount of money on real estate. I'll take real estate rather than go to Wall Street and get 2.8 percent. Forget about it.❞**
>
> Ivana Trump

Things changed after the world wars, as successive governments embarked on policies to find 'homes for heroes'. Controls were imposed on landlords and millions of pounds were poured into homebuilding projects. Meanwhile, inequality was falling, meaning that many more middle-class families were suddenly able to afford to buy a home.

Amid the post-war optimism of 1950s Britain, home ownership slowly but surely became enshrined as a talismanic social objective, along with free healthcare, free education and low unemployment. The apogee was Margaret Thatcher's right-to-buy scheme, which saw thousands of council tenants buying their homes.

All these factors contributed to a sharp rise in home ownership. One government after another introduced lucrative tax breaks on mortgages, with the result that owner occupancy soared, recently reaching an all-time peak of 70 per cent. It was one of the biggest social and economic transformations in British history.

The UK's relationship with housing is not unique. In terms of home ownership rates, Spain is further ahead while France is fast catching up. Significantly, it is usually only in countries with widespread home ownership that major housing booms and busts develop – so, for instance, countries such as Germany and Switzerland, where more people tend to rent than buy, have resisted these major bubbles. But this is due less to an ingrained cultural reticence about home-buying than to laws that make it more financially attractive to rent.

Economic dangers While there are undoubted social benefits to increasing home ownership, there are economic problems associated with it. For example, it overrules the so-called invisible hand of capitalism (see chapter 1). In a properly functioning market, when prices rise to what might be considered unreasonable levels people stop buying and prices fall back into a more sensible range. If, however, governments offer either home-buyers – or the mortgage companies that finance them – incentives to buy (through tax breaks or implicit guarantees of support), it makes bubbles more likely to form.

This is precisely what happened in the years that preceded 2007, as the two mortgage giants that underpinned the US home loans market, Fannie Mae and Freddie Mac, took ever-increasing risks with their lending. Most investors assumed that if the two collapsed they would be rescued by the government, and they were proved right when, in 2008, the government was forced to nationalize them. The question that remains is whether, in the future, US and UK mortgage lenders will have to do without government support and whether this would mean an end to housing bubbles and crashes.

Home ownership rates

Spain	85%
Ireland	77%
Norway	77%
UK	69%
US	69%
Austria	56%
France	55%
Germany	42%

the condensed idea
House prices go down as well as up

38 Government deficits

If there is one thing that recent times have taught us, it is that governments will borrow more and more each year. Barely a month goes by without an international institution such as the International Monetary Fund (IMF) or Organization for Economic Cooperation and Development (OECD) warning the United States and United Kingdom about the parlous state of their finances.

Indeed, in almost every year in post-war history, the US administration has recorded a *budget deficit* – in other words, it has received less in tax revenues than it has spent, and has had to borrow to make up the difference. It is not alone. The UK has also recorded a series of budget deficits (also known as *fiscal deficits*) in recent years, pushing its government finances further into the red.

> **❛As we have seen time after time in developing countries, unbridled government borrowing and spending produce hyperinflation and economic devastation. So deficits *must* matter.❜**
>
> Alan Greenspan, former Federal Reserve Chairman

It was not always this way. For most of the US's history – and for much of the UK's – governments kept the budgets balanced, plunging them into the red only in times of war and economic slump. There are also a number of countries that operate budget surpluses, including Norway (because of its prodigious oil reserves) and Australia (because of its metal resources).

Where does it all go? Although it is the subject of debate, most economists believe that the era of persistent government deficits began when the state started to provide extensive social security systems for their citizens. This involved spending massive amounts of money on, for instance, health, unemployment insurance and education, all of

timeline

1936	**1945**
Keynes argues in *The General Theory of Employment, Interest and Money* that governments should borrow more in times of recession	US total public debt touches 120 per cent of gross domestic produc following the Second World War

which tended previously to be handled by the private sector or by charities and trusts. It was a shift from a warfare state to a welfare state.

Where does the spending go? A quick look at the US Federal Budget for 2008 (see pie chart, right) shows that the vast majority of this is spent on so-called mandatory items – in other words, spending that the government is obliged to perform. This includes social security (mainly payments to the elderly), income security (payments to poor families), Medicare and other health payments, including Medicaid (respectively, government health spending for the elderly and the poor) and interest payments on the debt the government has taken out in previous years. By far the biggest chunk of the government's discretionary spending is on defence (salaries of servicemen and women, and equipment – from aircraft carriers to guns). The 'other' category includes spending on federal institutions such as the courts system, support for farmers and NASA.

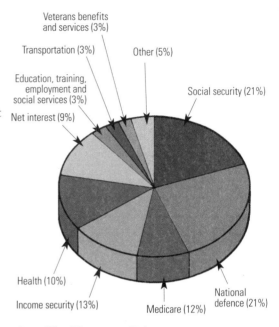

Veterans benefits and services (3%)
Transportation (3%)
Other (5%)
Education, training, employment and social services (3%)
Social security (21%)
Net interest (9%)
Health (10%)
Income security (13%)
Medicare (12%)
National defence (21%)

Source: Office of Management and Budget

The pie chart shows US government spending for 2008. The breakdown is very similar in most Western economies.

However, since the amount the US government spent in 2008 exceeded the amount it raised in taxes, it is having to make up the balance with some $410 billion worth of borrowing – a hefty amount.

On top of this, because of the Federal structure of US government, each state also has its own budget (and tax-raising abilities), most of which is spent on education and local infrastructure such as highways. Sometimes congressmen from particular states insert special additions to Federal bills to help pay for expensive local projects (even though the bill to which these flyers are attached might be completely unrelated). This is called 'pork barrel' politics and is another reason why the deficit has risen so sharply – particularly during the presidency of George W. Bush, who,

2009

President Barack Obama concedes that the US budget deficit will rise to $1 trillion as efforts continue to fight the financial crisis

Automatic stabilizers

Any modern state with a welfare system sees its budget deficit swing sharply into negative territory during a recession. The fall in profits and wages at such times means that companies and individuals pay less tax to the government. Simultaneously, the amount the government has to spend increases, since it has more laid-off workers to support through its unemployment support system. Government spending automatically helps 'stabilize' the economy, keeping people off the streets and safeguarding their welfare. In short, this is Keynesianism in action (see chapter 9).

For example, in the early 1990s, when the UK faced a serious downturn and housing-market slump, the deficit rose from 1 per cent of GDP to 7.3 per cent between 1990 and 1993. This happened because of the so-called *automatic stabilizers* inherent in the way modern budgets are structured.

unlike his predecessors, proved extremely reluctant to use his right to veto the bills. His successor Barack Obama pledged to reverse this in the future.

Ever-increasing shortfalls It is important to distinguish between the annual budget deficit and the total stock of outstanding government debt. As the annual deficits mount up they increase the overall amount owed by the government – often called the net debt. As of late 2008, the total US debt owned by the public was $5.3 trillion ($5,300,000 million), though this does not include the liabilities of Fannie Mae and Freddie Mac, the mortgage guarantee institutions bailed out by the government in September 2008, or indeed the banks it subsequently had to bring into temporary public ownership.

Both this and the budget deficits tend to rise each year. This is not necessarily a concern – provided the debt is not expanding much faster than the economy. This is why deficits and debt levels are often expressed as a percentage of a country's gross domestic product. The US public debt, for instance, was 37 per cent of GDP in late 2008. As a country's national debt increases, the amount it has to pay in interest payments also increases, with these repayments also being pushed up by higher interest rates.

Consequences of higher borrowing If deficits are allowed to run out of control, they can cause a variety of economic problems for a country. The first is that higher borrowing tends to weaken that country's currency.

In the UK in 2008, the pound weakened by almost one-fifth after investors judged that the government was set to borrow excessively in the coming years. The flight from a debtor country's currency is quite rational, since when a country gets into excessive indebtedness its response is invariably to inflate away that debt by printing more currency. Any hint that this might happen – which would erode the value of anything denominated in that currency – and foreign investors usually run a mile.

The other consequence is that investors will demand a higher rate of return on their investments to compensate them for this risk. This pushes up the interest rate that the government has to pay on its debt, making it more costly to borrow in the future.

Most fundamental, however, are the long-term consequences of borrowing too highly. Effectively, government borrowing is merely deferred taxation from future years, since the extra borrowed money has to be paid back at some point in the future. This is not a problem if the money is being used to enhance future generations' welfare, such as investing in building new schools, but it is a real cause for concern if the money is merely being used to satisfy the public sector's current appetite for cash.

Breaking the Golden Rule This is why a number of countries have set themselves fiscal rules to ensure that future generations do not have to bear the cost of current borrowing. A good example is the Golden Rule set up in the UK by former Chancellor of the Exchequer Gordon Brown. He pledged to borrow money only for use on investment in public projects, and never to fund current spending, such as state workers' salaries.

However, the rule ran into trouble in late 2008 as it became clear that the government would have to borrow extensively in the face of recession. It was a phenomenon mirrored across the world, and it underlined the enduring truth about public finances: governments keep borrowing until markets or voters prevent them from doing so.

the condensed idea
Governments are addicted to debt

39 Inequality

If you were to walk down the beach in Rio de Janeiro, past Ipanema and Leblon, you would come across some of the finest villas in Brazil. These lavish multi-million-dollar palaces have a wealth of luxurious components – fully equipped cinemas, tennis courts, swimming pools, jacuzzis and servants' quarters. And yet only yards away sits one of the largest and most lawless shantytowns in the world. How can such acute poverty exist alongside so much plenty?

Inequality is nothing new. In Victorian England it was particularly severe, rich industrialists amassing unprecedented fortunes while the average working family was forced to endure immense hardship working in mills and mines and living in houses not altogether dissimilar to those shantytowns of Brazil.

Despite politicians' continued efforts to reduce the gap between rich and poor, the divide remains intractably high. In the two and a half decades since the early 1980s, levels of inequality have, in fact, widened significantly in almost every developed country around the world. Although the gap decreased in France, Greece and Spain, the poverty divide worsened significantly in the UK, and towards the end of the first decade of the new millennium, both in the UK and in the US, inequality hit the highest level since the 1930s.

Wealth gaps Given that capitalism is a system that rewards individuals' hard work and entrepreneurship, it is hardly surprising that some will be richer than others – after all, what incentive would there be to work hard

timeline

1840s

Levels of inequality in industrial England inspire Friedrich Engels to write *The Condition of the Working Class in England*

1930

Inequality in the US reaches record highs

unless it offers some sort of reward? However, what has become alarming is the sheer size of the disparity. In the US the richest one-tenth have around 16 times bigger incomes than the poorest tenth, while the rich in Mexico, which has shantytowns as squalid as those in Rio, are more than 25 times wealthier than the poor.

Meanwhile, in Nordic countries such as Denmark, Sweden and Finland, the gap is far smaller, with the wealthiest earning around five times the amount that the poorest earn. These wealth gaps are calculated using something called the 'gini coefficient', which is a comparison of income between the top earners and those at the bottom of the pile.

The disparity is wider still when one compares levels of wealth in different countries. By most yardsticks, the poorest fifth of the world's population – those mainly in sub-Saharan Africa – still live in the economic equivalent of the Middle Ages, while even the poorest in the UK and US are incomparably wealthier and healthier.

> **'A society that puts equality before freedom will get neither. A society that puts freedom before equality will get a high degree of both.'**
>
> **Milton Friedman**

The redistribution dividend There are some clear explanations for these disparities. Nordic countries – and many Northern European ones – tend to tax their citizens more heavily in order to redistribute money to the poor, through social-welfare schemes and tax breaks. This is one of the main objectives of tax systems in modern democracies – to reduce unfairness and help support those citizens who find themselves in need.

As rich countries around the world constructed their respective welfare systems in the post-war years, levels of inequality dropped significantly. By offering all families similar access to education and healthcare, many countries – particularly the Nordics – succeeded in equalizing the opportunities available to families. It is what is often referred to as the 'Swedish Model' of running a country.

1950s	**1990s**	**2000s**
Wealth divide narrows, partly as a result of Franklin D. Roosevelt's New Deal	Gap increases in the wake of Thatcherism and Reaganism	Inequality hits new peaks

The benefits of inequality

Some economists argue that, since people are innately different in terms of their habits and capabilities, a certain amount of inequality is inevitable in a major economy. Indeed, those who favour free markets argue that attempts to redistribute wealth have perverse unintended consequences. Higher taxes can drive the most productive members of society overseas, or can discourage them from working harder, which in turn reduces the amount of wealth generated overall by society.

However, raising taxes on the rich in order to give more to the poor is not enough by itself. In the UK, the Labour government elected in 1997 did precisely this, so that the average lone parent saw his or her income rise by 11 per cent over its first decade in power. And yet, at the same time, inequality rose to the highest level in recent decades. Worse still, a study from the Organization for Economic Cooperation and Development (OECD) found that a son's income was closely tied to his father's, implying that youngsters had few opportunities to break free of poverty.

Driving the difference The world is in the midst of a major shift in its economic structure, as companies capitalize on new technologies such as the Internet and advanced computing and telecommunications. When these shifts happen it often pushes up inequality, those prepared for the shift becoming wealthy while those who aren't – for instance, a Detroit car worker – finding themselves left behind. It is what happened in the Industrial Revolution and it is also happening now.

Another explanation is that a very small number of people have managed to become super-rich. In the UK, for instance, whereas the 3 million people that make up the top one-tenth of workers earn an average of £105,000 before tax, the top 0.1 per cent, or 30,000 people, have an average annual income of £1.1 million. These super-wealthy are often able to avoid paying significant amounts of tax by moving their wealth offshore to tax havens, meaning that less cash is redistributed. On the flip-side, these wealthy families can contribute to the economy through the indirect taxes they pay when they spend extravagantly on luxury goods, and by employing local workers – ranging from cleaners and maids to stylists and lawyers. This is often known as the 'trickle-down' effect.

The consequences of inequality There is no clear sign that, taken as a whole, a high level of inequality prevents a country from becoming wealthier over time. Indeed, prominent economist Robert Barro found that, while it seems to reduce growth in the developing world, inequality actually boosts growth in the developed world.

However, a gaping wealth divide can be damaging for a country in other ways. The main point of concern is that of social unrest. Studies show that in countries and areas where income inequality is small, people are more likely to trust each other, which makes sense, given that people there will generally have less reason to envy others. Violent and fatal crimes are also far less frequent. For example, there is a strong correlation between US states with a high wealth divide and a high incidence of homicides.

Low incomes are also closely associated with poor health. In Glasgow, Scotland, where the gap between rich and poor is particularly acute, the average male's life expectancy is worse than in much of the developing world, including Algeria, Egypt, Turkey and Vietnam.

Such inequality issues are not merely to be found in economics. People derive their sense of self-worth, which feeds into their personal productivity, largely from how they view themselves in comparison to others. When people are aware of their income deficit in relation to others, they will tend to be less contented and strive less hard.

A study has found that Hollywood actors who won an Academy Award lived on average four years longer than their non-winning counterparts, and double Oscar-winners an extra six years. Being rewarded for one's hard work really does make a difference. Whether it hits your pride or your purse, inequality matters.

the condensed idea
The wealth gap will destabilize nations

40 Globalization

Just as capitalism was originally designed as a term of abuse rather than of praise or mere description, globalization is more often used to criticize than eulogize the 21st-century world economy. It summons up images of sweatshops in Malaysia, call centres in Bangalore, mines in Brazil, and of branches of Starbucks and McDonald's all over the world.

All of the above are a consequence of globalization, but to describe the phenomenon in such terms alone would be highly misleading. In economics, globalization refers to the commercial and economic links that straddle the world and that have done so for much of human history.

As old as the hills? Globalization has been growing in importance since 1492, the year Columbus made landfall in the Americas, though there was vibrant international trade between Europe and the East long before that. Although use of the term has been prevalent since the 1980s, and although the decades following the fall of the Berlin Wall and the end of the Cold War are widely regarded as a high-water mark for globalization, this is far from being the first era of widespread international trade, commerce and migration. That accolade must go the Victorian age. In the late 19th century, as the British empire reached its apex, John Maynard Keynes described how, prior to 1914:

> The inhabitant of London could order by telephone, sipping his morning tea, the various products of the whole earth, and reasonably expect their early delivery upon his doorstep; he could at the same moment and by the same means adventure his wealth in the natural resources and new enterprises of any quarter of the world, and share . . . in their prospective fruits and advantages . . .

timeline

1800s	1914
First era of globalization	First World War brings the first era to an end

It was not just the First World War but also the period of protectionism following the Great Depression that brought an end to this era. Many fear that this modern age of globalization could meet a similarly miserable end.

Key factors behind globalization There are five key factors behind recent globalization:

1. *Free trade.* Governments worldwide have torn down a number of major barriers and tariffs on imports and exports. For instance, after adopting free-market reforms in the late 1980s and early 1990s, China removed many retrictions on its export markets. Because of its mammoth population, and therefore low wages, this meant an influx into rich nations of cheap goods emanating from China and its neighbours.

> **‘Globalization is a fact of life. But I believe we have underestimated its fragility.’**
>
> **Kofi Annan**

2. *Outsourcing.* Companies have been able to save money by shifting production of their goods and services to cheaper locations overseas. Many manufacturers have shut down their plants in the US and UK and relocated them to China, Mexico and elsewhere, where workers accept lower wages and – controversially – working conditions are frequently poor. Many service companies have relocated their call centres, and even parts of their main business, to India and elsewhere, where fluent English-speaking graduates are plentiful.

3. *The communications revolution.* Two major revolutions have greased the wheels of international commerce. The first was 'containerization' – the breakthrough in shipping whereby goods are now transported worldwide in standard-sized containers, cutting costs and improving transit time. The second was the broadband breakthrough. As the Internet boom hit its peak in the late 1990s engineers spent billions on a new international fibre-optic network of cables. Although the dot-com bubble burst soon afterwards, this global web of information superhighways brought fast and cheap Internet connection to millions.

4. *Liberalization.* Many countries which, during the Cold War, had tended

1980s	**1989**	**2007**
First studies of economic globalization	World Wide Web is developed by Tim Berners-Lee	A UN report reveals that flows of trade and investment worldwide have hit a record peak

to keep their borders closed to foreign contacts, were encouraged to open them. This allowed Western companies to enter new markets. The elimination of so-called capital controls meant money could flow freely in and out of these new, younger economies in a way it had never done before. Meanwhile, governments in the developed world made it easier for firms to hire and fire workers by relaxing labour laws.

5. *Legal harmonization.* Countries around the world have made efforts to align their laws on property rights and intellectual property so that, for instance, a patent filed in the US will be recognized in China and vice versa. Future plans include laying down international standards for the quality of goods, to avoid recurrences of recent incidents in which products from China and elsewhere were found to have potentially dangerous defects.

Gains of globalization Globalization has without doubt made billions around the world significantly richer. The economies of countries such as Brazil, India and China have been boosted by massive leaps in their exports. In addition, the entrance of this new band of exporters pushed down inflation around the world for almost a decade from 1997 onwards, as companies took advantage of the opportunity to cut costs and passed on the resulting savings to their customers.

Indeed, there is much evidence to suggest that globalization was largely responsible for what has become known as the 'Great Stability' for the fifteen or so years up until 2007. During that period, the world economy grew faster and for a longer stretch than ever before, and inflation remained low and stable. True, this was followed by a major financial crisis, but that was largely due to other factors (see chapter 35).

Criticisms of globalization The faster the tenets of globalization have spread throughout the world, the louder and more strident have become the criticisms. Meetings of the major multilateral institutions regularly draw thousands of protestors. The World Trade Organization's meeting in Cancun in 2003, for example, was marred by the suicide of a South Korean farmer over the removal of agricultural support.

Opponents of globalization, who include Naomi Klein, Joseph Stiglitz and Noam Chomsky, sometimes label its most ardent proponents neoliberalists. They attack the phenomenon largely from three angles:

1. *Economic.* They argue that although globalization has pushed up the total amount of wealth generated around the world, that wealth has not been evenly shared. Indeed, inequality levels around the world have risen to their highest levels since the 1930s (see chapter 39), and while some have become billionaires thanks to global trade many in the poorest countries remain extremely poor.
2. *Human Rights.* Some major clothing and footwear manufacturers have come under fire for using sweatshops where employees are paid extremely low wages and forced to work in appalling conditions for long stretches.
3. *Cultural.* Critics argue that the increased influence of multinational corporations, and the increasing dominance of Western brands, have made it hard for indigenous cultures to retain their identities and caused smaller independent shops and producers to be elbowed aside.

An era of peace and democracy? Despite the manifold criticisms of globalization, the evidence shows that, on balance, it has dramatically improved standards of living in those countries that have embraced it – though, as ever in capitalism, the gains are not evenly distributed. Moreover, the fact that it boosts the fortunes of the middle and professional classes suggests that it may also aid the spread of democracy. Political strategists suspect that the Communist Party may struggle to maintain its grip on power in China as popular demands for democratic rule, fuelled by the growing influence of the middle classes, increase in volume.

Another argument in favour of globalization is that stronger economic links between nations tend to deter them from going to war with one another. Thomas Friedman, the US journalist and author of the paean to globalization, *The World is Flat*, posited that no two countries with a McDonald's had ever been to war with one another. However, such an assertion was disproved when Russia waged war on Georgia in 2008. And the lesson from the first era of globalization, which came to a nasty end with the First World War, is that you can never assume the spread of trade and wealth has changed the world forever.

the condensed idea
Globalization is the adrenaline of capitalism

41 Multilateralism

The years since the turn of the millennium have witnessed one of the biggest ever shifts in global economic power. The tectonic plates underlying the world economy started to move – more quickly than most have ever witnessed. As a new breed of contenders emerged – led by China and India – it appeared as if the United States was losing its status as the world's undisputed superpower. In the past, such moments have frequently sparked geopolitical instability, but economists hope that, this time around, a secret weapon will avert conflict: *multilateralism*.

Multilateralism means collaborating with all other major countries when taking major decisions, rather than a country acting on its own – unilaterally – or in partnership with just one other country (or set of countries) – bilaterally. It seems like common sense, but, even in an era of globalization, economic nationalism is a powerful force.

> **❝By virtue of exchange, one man's prosperity is beneficial to all others.❞**
>
> Frédéric Bastiat, 19th-century French economist

Often, when a country decides to raise tariffs on trade, or to artificially inflate the value of its currency, it sets off a chain reaction that can cause major damage to other countries. For instance, the 1990s and first decade of the new millennium were characterized by developed countries allowing their exchange rates to float and many Asian and Middle Eastern nations fixing their currencies against the dollar. While this allowed the developing countries to grow a little faster (since it kept their exports cheap) it also led, eventually, to a massive build-up of debt in the rich world, which in turn contributed to the 2008 financial crisis.

timeline

1944	**1945**
Bretton Woods Conference – IMF and World Bank founded	United Nations is established

It was to try to avoid such issues that politicians from around the world developed multilateral institutions. The first was the League of Nations, which was masterminded by President Woodrow Wilson after the First World War and which later transformed itself into the United Nations. However, it is the crop of economic multilateral institutions that sprouted up after the Second World War which have come to dominate the interrelationships between modern economies in recent years.

The children of Bretton Woods At the Bretton Woods Conference in the United States in 1944, held in the opulent Mount Washington Hotel, politicians from around the world, under the tutelage of John Maynard Keynes, sat down to create a new financial and economic architecture for the post-war world. Alongside a system of fixed currency rates, they created two major institutions: the International Monetary Fund (IMF), and the predecessor to today's World Bank, the International Bank for Reconstruction and Development. They also set up the General Agreement on Tariffs and Trade (GATT), which later metamorphosed into the World Trade Organization (WTO).

Between them, these multilateral organizations, whose membership now includes every country in the world except a few despotic regimes, still determine the shape of the global economy and the way countries interact with each other.

The IMF acts as the world's central bank, pooling resources from its members and lending out cash to those who suffer a major currency or capital account (see chapter 24) crisis. It is a lender of last resort – but in this case to countries rather than banks and companies. Its second role is to ensure that countries around the world are running their economies sensibly, without brewing up problems for the future. However, having no 'teeth' – no power to discipline those who defy it – it has failed, in the past, to prevent some countries taking poor economic decisions.

1989
Fall of Berlin Wall

2008
The G7 is replaced with the G20

The BRICs

The BRICs are an idea, a phenomenon and a quartet of the world's most up-and-coming countries: Brazil, Russia, India and China. If the 20th-century economy was dominated by the G7, the 21st is surely set to be dominated by the BRICs. Their massive populations, incredible appetite for work and prodigious growth means that they are already responsible for around half the world's economic growth in recent years. The man who coined the term, Goldman Sachs's chief economist Jim O'Neill, calculated that China was growing so fast that by the mid-21st century it would overtake the US as the world's biggest economy.

Together, Brazil, Russia, India and China account for 40 per cent of the world's population and more than one-quarter of its landmass. Their economies are growing at rates of 10 per cent, or perhaps more, compared with Western economies which tend to expand at one-quarter of that speed. As the world's workshops, they are pumping out billions of dollars' worth of exports each day, to rich nations and each other.

The World Trade Organization is both a forum in which countries agree on removing trade barriers and an arbiter when one country suspects another of illegally imposing extra tariffs or quotas on their goods. It advocates reduced trade barriers throughout the world.

The World Bank is designed to provide assistance to the world's most impoverished countries. By lending – and in some cases donating – cash to troubled economies, the Bank's aim is to make the world economy richer and more stable. However, it has come under fire for imposing tough conditions on those to whom it hands out cash – a criticism also levelled at the IMF.

No consensus Throughout the 1990s the IMF and World Bank tended to try to impose policies that would remould other economies according to their own ideals. This became known as the Washington Consensus. The prescription, which included cutting budget deficits and pulling down barriers on their domestic markets, has been described by Harvard economist Dani Rodrik as 'stabilize, privatize and liberalize'. The problem was that many economies simply could not cope with the massive influx of cash from overseas when they opened up their markets to foreign investors.

Since the end of the Cold War and following the financial crisis of 2008, the institutions faced mounting criticism for their failure to prevent repeated economic crises in various parts of the world. The attitude towards them of the US, in particular, has become increasingly cold, with calls for major reform – particularly at the IMF and World Bank.

Among the concerns is that the IMF is not representative enough of the new fast-growing world economic powers. Until recently, China – which has grown so fast that it is now close to becoming the world's third-biggest economy – had only the same number of votes at the IMF as Belgium.

From G7 to G20 The same criticism has been levelled against the G7 – the group of the world's seven major industrialized economies. This group – which comprised the United States, Japan, Germany, the UK, France, Italy and Canada – was a fair representation of the world's major powers between the 1970s and 1990s. Whenever there was an international economic summit it was dominated by the G7, whose members made the big decisions in concert with one another.

However, in 2008, when President George W. Bush called a special summit to discuss the mounting financial crisis, it became clear that countries such as China, Brazil, Russia and India needed to be included. So the G7 was replaced with the G20 – a far broader group of the world's largest economies.

The hope is that by cooperating with each other multilaterally, the members (19 countries plus the European Union) will be able to manage the move from a world with one economic superpower to a world with two or more.

the condensed idea
Nations can achieve more by working together

42 Protectionism

Back in the 1980s, as American citizens were fretting about Japan's increasing dominance in global commerce, members of Congress called a press conference on the steps of the Senate and symbolically smashed a Toshiba radio to pieces. A few years later, in the 1990s, politicians warned of a 'giant sucking sound' as American jobs went south following the removal of trade barriers with Mexico. A decade later still, lawmakers banned a Chinese takeover of a US oil company and a Middle Eastern takeover of the US wing of a ports group. Why is it that protectionism – globalization's ugly sister – retains such an enduring grasp on the modern world?

Protectionism – which usually means the imposition of high barriers and tariffs on goods imported from overseas, and the prevention of foreign takeovers – is as old as trade itself. One of the earliest methods that rulers found of raising money was to slap tariffs on trade – something that has endured since ancient times.

These days, ways of protecting an economy include: quotas on the quantity or value of goods being imported; subsidies for producers – a notorious example being Europe's Common Agricultural Policy, which provides handouts for farmers; subsidies for exporters; manipulating the exchange rate to keep the currency low and make exports more attractive than imports; and extra bureaucracy. Another type of protectionism, seen in the financial and economic crisis that began in 2008, involved banks lending only to companies from their own country. It was described by British Prime Minister Gordon Brown in 2009 as 'financial mercantilism', but he

timeline

c1798	1930
US President George Washington constructs earliest American tariffs, on trade with the UK	The US adopts protectionist tariffs, including the Smoot-Hawley Act, which raises barriers to foreign trade

too was guilty of the sin, encouraging UK banks to favour British customers when lending out new cash, rather than their clients overseas.

For and against Almost all economists abhor protectionism, and favour its opposite, free trade. They warn that constructing such barriers makes us all poorer in the long run, causes bitter political friction, and can even spark wars. It is, they warn, among the most damaging of all economic policies.

Such arguments are supported by comparative advantage (see chapter 7) – the theory that shows how, by specializing in certain products and trading with other countries, each separate country can become more prosperous, even if they are less efficient at producing goods than their neighbours.

Politically, however, the issues are more complex. Say, for instance, that a US factory faces closure because its overseas competitors can produce goods far more cheaply. An economist would argue that the market is issuing a clear signal: the US factory can no longer compete and should be shut down. A protectionist, on the other hand, would recommend increasing tariffs on those goods and perhaps pumping subsidies into the sector, to save jobs. Such an option is likely to win popular support – certainly among the workers. However, economics shows that it would simply mask the problem, which

Round and round

The World Trade Organization (WTO) is the organization charged with leading the fight against protectionism. The primary role of the institution, which evolved from the post-war General Agreement on Tariffs and Trade, is to bring countries together to discuss how to remove tariffs and barriers on trade. These talks must be global, since only by removing tariffs internationally rather than unilaterally can all countries benefit.

In the early 1990s, the WTO clinched the Uruguay Round of multilateral talks, which succeeded in dismantling major trade barriers worldwide and is credited with helping boost economic growth throughout the following decade. However, the Doha Round, which began in 2001, suffered a number of major setbacks as countries quarrelled over their contributions. In summer 2008, the talks were suspended as the US clashed with China, India and Brazil over the scale of cuts it was prepared to make to its farming subsidies. Although some hope the talks may be resumed, many warn they are now as good as dead.

1994

World Trade Organization signs off the Uruguay Round, dismantling trade barriers

2008

Doha Round of trade talks is suspended

would inevitably soon resurface. Better, the economist would say, for the laid-off workers to find new jobs in another, more competitive industry.

Not only is protectionism the easier policy to sell to voters, it can also show superficial signs of success. If a government imposes tariffs, revenues may rise initially thanks to the extra money these bring in, while domestic companies enjoy a boom as consumers are encouraged to buy home-produced goods rather than those from overseas counterparts. More compelling still for those of a patriotic (or nationalist) bent is that protectionism can apparently secure the country's independence, whether in the production of energy, steel, cars, computers or whatever. It also plays to the knee-jerk perception that a country becomes poorer when one of its domestic firms is taken over by an international rival.

The problem, however, is that such arguments are largely misguided. Study after study has shown that, in the long run, protectionism makes countries poor – both the nation with the tariffs and those who would like to trade with it.

Lessons from history The most potent example of what protectionism can lead to is from the 1930s, when – in the thick of the Great Depression – countries around the world, including the US, constructed major barriers to trade, in the belief that these would safeguard domestic jobs and help their economies recover more quickly. These were dubbed 'beggar-thy-neighbour' policies, since they left many countries, which had relied on trade with foreign partners, in dire straits. As country after country erected their own tariffs in response, world trade effectively froze, worsening political tensions and contributing to the breakdown of relations that triggered the Second World War.

> **❛When goods cannot cross borders, armies will.❜**
> Frédéric Bastiat,
> 19th-century
> French economist

It was only when these barriers started to be dismantled in the wake of the Second World War that comparative advantage once again came to the fore, contributing to a blistering period of world growth in the 1950s and 1960s as each economy specialized in producing certain goods. It was freer trade than ever before.

Another example is China, which fell victim to a destructive trade policy in the 15th century. At the time, it was among the world's most advanced and wealthiest economies, but its rulers embarked on a policy of autarky (economic self-sufficiency), cutting off most of its economic and cultural ties with the rest of the world, and it swiftly lost its pre-eminence. It was only late in the 20th century, when it cut many of its tariffs and trade barriers, that the country once again began to realize its massive economic potential.

> **❝If there were an Economist's Creed, it would surely contain the affirmations "I believe in the Principle of Comparative Advantage" and "I believe in Free Trade".❞**
>
> **Paul Krugman, Nobel laureate and trade expert**

Protecting jobs? Despite some people's fears, it is not necessarily true that breaking down barriers on trade means that jobs will be 'sucked out' of the economy. One of Britain's biggest and most efficient car factories is run not by a British or even European company but by Japanese motor manufacturer Nissan. It employs thousands of workers in the north-east of England, an area of high unemployment. True, there are concerns that foreign companies, when they need to cut costs, may be quicker to cut jobs from their overseas plants rather than at home, but there is little statistical evidence to back this up.

The fundamental problem is that protecting an economy's businesses from foreign competition makes them less competitive, discouraging them from cutting costs and improving their efficiency. Indeed, experts argue that, given how hard it is for shareholders to eject a poorly performing chief executive from a company, the threat of a foreign takeover is one of the key checks to ensure management works hard at improving its business.

A protectionist relapse? As countries attempt to repair their economies following the financial crisis of 2008, some fear it will lead to a new spate of protectionism across the globe. In fact, many experts believe that this, rather than the threat of depression and debt deflation, remains the biggest threat to the global economy over the next decade. As history has shown, it is all too easy to become trapped in a protectionist spiral, with horrifying consequences for world peace and stability.

the condensed idea
The biggest threat to world peace and prosperity

43 Technological revolutions

Apt as we are to romanticize it, life in 18th-century England was hardly Arcadian. Most families were trapped in a subsistence existence, barely earning enough to survive. A staggering three-quarters of children born in London died before the age of five. But between around 1750 and the early 19th century, everything changed radically. Life expectancy shot up, as did the population and its wealth. Few economic periods were more epochal than that of the Industrial Revolution.

New technology lay behind the transformation. The invention of the steam engine and the exploitation of fossil fuels such as coal suddenly changed the way people lived, reshaping social and artistic horizons. It was the era of Wordsworth and Turner, of both artistic horror and delight at the profound changes taking place; and a period of political insecurity that coincided with the French Revolution and the achievement of American independence.

However, this most famous sea change was not the only economic revolution in history. Across the centuries, humankind has advanced in sporadic leaps and bounds as new technologies have been devised. Often the jumps have been entirely unexpected, but they trigger radical changes in human prosperity and interaction.

Economic historians identify not just one but *three* industrial revolutions since the 18th century – what they see as *structural* rather than *cyclical*

timeline

1600	1756	1778
British East India Company is founded	Rediscovery of concrete	The Iron Bridge is built in Shropshire and James Watt perfects his steam engine

shifts; in other words, changes in the very foundations of the economy rather than routine ebb and flow.

The first industrial revolution The *first industrial revolution* stretched from the mid-1700s – and the invention of the steam engine – to the early 19th century. Prior to this period, humans were reliant on nature – the power of wind, water or of animals such as horses and oxen – for their survival. Subsequently, they could harness coal to drive machinery, which increased productivity. Humans then mastered the creation of metal machinery, which gave rise to the first true factories – the grand embodiment of Adam Smith's division of labour (see chapter 6). At first, the revolution occurred in England, but it soon spread throughout Europe and then to America.

The effects of the revolution were profound. Until then, gross domestic product per head in the UK – a measure of wealth creation (see chapter 17) – had been static since before the Middle Ages. Suddenly it leapt dramatically higher. In the eyes of some economists, this was when Western economies escaped from the Malthusian trap (see chapter 3), in which the limits of population consigned them to stagnant growth. As wealth and life expectancy increased, so did the size of the average family,

> **The fundamental impulse that sets the capitalist engine in motion comes from the new consumers' goods, the new methods of production or transportation, and new markets, and the new forms of industrial organization that capitalist enterprise creates.**
>
> **Joseph Schumpeter**

1885
First automobile powered by internal combustion engine is invented by Karl Benz in Germany

1903
Wright brothers fly the first powered plane

1989
World Wide Web is developed by Tim Berners-Lee

Leapfrog technologies

Among the undoubted hallmarks of progress, if not revolution, are what are known as *leapfrog technologies*. Many parts of the world originally owe their prosperity to expensive infrastructure – for instance, the rails for a railway or power lines for an electricity network. Parts of the world without that legacy of infrastructure simply could not develop as rapidly. However, the mobile phone has brought telephony to vast stretches of Africa where it would previously have been uneconomical to build a network. Small solar power plants also promise to do similar, providing power for communities that have never previously benefited from electricity. Whether this spells, as some suspect, a gradual move around the world to less centralized cities and communities remains to be seen, though environmentalists believe it may be an answer to pollution and climate change (see chapter 45).

and the population of England and Wales rose from around 6 million in the 18th century to over 30 million by the end of the 19th.

The second industrial revolution The *second industrial revolution*, sometimes referred to as the electric or technical revolution, saw humankind develop metallurgy (creating steel and other metals), harness electricity, and exploit crude oil to create petroleum and gasoline. It was this age – an extension of the first revolution – that brought the world the motor car and the aeroplane, as well as the international corporation and the telephone. The era also saw Britain starting to lose its global influence, as the US and Germany rose rapidly to take their positions as budding global economic superpowers.

The third industrial revolution – the computer age Such have been recent advances in technology that many economists identify a *third industrial revolution*, stretching back to the late 1980s – a revolution brought about by the development of the computer and, just as importantly, the Internet, which has revolutionized global communication and commerce. In the 21st century it has become possible to transfer vast amounts of capital (wealth and assets) from one side of the world to another with just the press of a button. Companies can outsource entire divisions of their businesses to India, China or elsewhere because of advances in broadband communication, enabling them to save billions and boost their profits.

As with previous revolutions, this technological leap has coincided with the ascendancy of new potential superpowers keen to capitalize on the shift – in this case China and India. In the decade leading up to 2006 the rise of these countries coupled with technological revolution contributed towards the longest period of world economic growth on record. Although the global economy subsequently slid into a sharp recession, most economists believe that the third industrial revolution will continue to yield rewards in the coming decades.

While there was certainly a technological leap, some doubt that the new Internet economy represents as significant a shift as those seen in previous revolutions. Profound though recent changes have been, they have not – according to economist Robert Gordon of Northwestern University – had such a deep impact on people's lives as earlier innovations, such as electricity, mass transportation, cinema, radio and indoor plumbing.

Future revolutions The computer age may only be the herald of a revolution that transforms human beings themselves. There is much evidence to suggest that the recent decoding of the human genome may lead to major advances in human capability. In a prospective bio-revolution, humans may soon be able to wield control over their genetic make-up, and while activities such as human cloning remain highly controversial, some suspect that therein may lie an opportunity for humankind to advance economically in the future.

Few people foresaw the revolutionary capacity of the computer or quite how radically the Internet would change the world economy. The likelihood is that further technological advances will make tomorrow's world almost completely unrecognizable.

the condensed idea
Technology is economic fuel

44 Development economics

The fall of the Berlin Wall and the collapse of communism in the old Soviet bloc was undoubtedly one of the most significant catalysts for economic growth throughout the world. It became clear that the command economy of the former Soviet Union had suppressed growth, impoverished millions and left many Russians starving and helpless. Now, as former communist states embraced the free market, their economies took off rapidly and, while some were left behind, millions became far wealthier.

However, there was a flip-side to this happy story. One of the by-products of the Cold War was that both sides had had little choice but to treat the poorer nations of the world (the developing, or Third World) kindly. They had drizzled wealth on them for fear of losing their favour. This meant that, all too often, Russia or the West helped support corrupt dictators, such as President Mobutu in Zaire or Augusto Pinochet in Chile, and the competition for favour ensured that cash kept flowing to these countries.

A new world That flow dried up very suddenly with the fall of the Iron Curtain. Many countries that had previously benefited from the flow of aid to support their economies (even if much of it had been siphoned off into their dictators' Swiss bank accounts) slumped further into poverty. This was not the case everywhere though. Indeed, liberation from strict communist or socialist economic controls helped China and much of East

timeline

1800s	1990
Life expectancy in the West vaults ahead during the Industrial Revolution	Fall of the Soviet Union sets China and India on the road to wealth

Asia to effect rapid economic growth, pulling millions out of poverty. The picture of the world changed.

No longer was it simply a case of the global economy being one-fifth rich and four-fifths poor. The new world consists of one-fifth rich economies; three-fifths emerging, industrializing and fast catching up; and one-fifth poor. Development economics is concerned largely with the plight of that final fifth or, in the words of Paul Collier (one of the world's leading experts in the field), the 'bottom billion'.

What makes a country rich? There are plenty of theories as to why some countries can so easily surmount poverty while others remain trapped in it. Some focus on the country's climate and topography, both of which can make it difficult to grow crops and develop farming; others on cultural mores such as its treatment of property rights; and others again on the success or failure of political and social institutions. For some, a country's wealth or otherwise is an accident of history; for others, it's a matter of destiny. A few less obvious factors have also been suggested. Biologist and anthropologist Jared Diamond, for example, believes that a resistance to certain diseases is an essential precondition for development, while economist Gregory Clark claims that class and the dissemination of hard-working middle-class culture or genes throughout society are key factors.

Either way, the fact is that in the Middle Ages there was very little meaningful difference in wealth between what are now termed the developed and developing worlds. Between then and now, a vast gulf

The Millennium Development Goals

The Millennium Development Goals (MDGs) are a set of eight goals focused on improving the plight of those living in developing nations. They were laid down by the United Nations in 2001, and are intended to be attained by 2015. However, in 2009, more than halfway towards the deadline, campaigners warned that progress was too slow.

- **Goal 1:** Eradicate extreme poverty and hunger
- **Goal 2:** Achieve universal primary education
- **Goal 3:** Promote gender equality and empower women
- **Goal 4:** Reduce child mortality
- **Goal 5:** Improve maternal health
- **Goal 6:** Combat HIV/AIDS, malaria and other diseases
- **Goal 7:** Ensure environmental sustainability
- **Goal 8:** Develop a Global Partnership for Development

2001
UN lays down the Millennium Development Goals

2015
Target date for the realization of the MDGs

> **'Before [the end of the Cold War] there had been the challenge from Russia that you'd better treat the developing countries reasonably well or they might go to the other side – so there was competition.'**
>
> Joseph Stiglitz, Nobel Prize-winner and former chief economist at the World Bank

opened up, and at the heart of this gulf is Africa. In economic terms, the continent remains stuck in medieval times. Most of sub-Saharan Africa is dominated by subsistence farming, with mortality rates worse in many cases than in pre-Reformation Europe. In recent years these have been exacerbated by the spread of AIDS throughout the continent, so that the average life expectancy among the world's poorest sixth is just 50 years, with one in seven children dying before the age of five.

The traps According to Collier, poor countries can fall into four traps, all of which prove immensely difficult to surmount:

1. *Civil war.* This afflicts almost three-quarters of those in the bottom billion. Examples include Angola, where half a million people lost their lives, and the Democratic Republic of Congo, which has been mired in more or less permanent civil war since 1997.

2. *Resource trap.* A country that discovers large reserves of natural resources – such as oil, gold or diamonds – within its borders is similarly vulnerable, as corrupt leaders are afforded even more opportunity to cling on to power and prevent the cash trickling down to the poor.

3. *Land trap.* Those without a sea border can find themselves vulnerable to the whims of their neighbours, which strangles trade and hence their economies.

4. *Bad governance.* Simply put, this means poor leadership and corruption from the leaders who have been elected or have forced their way into power.

What is to be done? Since the Cold War, a massive apparatus of institutions aimed at lifting the developing world out of poverty has emerged. This includes everything from development ministries in rich countries, multilateral institutions such as the World Bank and United Nations (see chapter 41), and non-governmental organizations (NGOs) such as Oxfam and Christian Aid.

The approach taken to the problem has changed over time. Rich countries and individuals tended in the past to give directly to the troubled countries, but dictators often funnelled such cash into their slush funds rather than spending it on health and education. These days aid agencies either spend the cash directly 'in the field' or attempt to attach conditions to the money, stipulating that it must be used for particular projects, ranging from providing families with mosquito nets and textbooks, to building schools, roads and bridges.

However, the problem facing the development community – one voiced by US economist William Easterly – is that these donations do little to equip nations for the transition from poverty to industrialization. China was a recipient of aid for many years, but such help had little, if anything, to do with its phenomenal growth from the 1990s onwards.

One solution to poverty in African countries is to allow them to trade with rich nations without having to pay tariffs on their exports. Another is to allow them to construct temporary barriers on imports to ensure that their manufacturing industries are not crowded out by those in China and elsewhere.

Ironically, part of the answer to the development crisis may lie with none other than China itself, for, having built up its riches so successfully in the early years of the new millennium, the giant Asian economy's donations to African states are now among the fastest growing in the world. Whether it ties this money to conditions that will genuinely help the most troubled nations escape the poverty trap is another question.

the condensed idea
Aim to pull the bottom billion out of poverty

45 Environmental economics

Economics and the environment are inextricably intertwined. Economic development, for example, is one of the prime reasons for climate change, but it could also conjure up its solution. Similarly, the study of economics is at the very forefront of investigations into global warming, and it is economic tools – such as taxes and regulation – that will most likely encourage people to pollute less in the future.

Humankind's economic evolution has gone hand in hand with exploiting the earth's natural resources, particularly since the Industrial Revolution. Without the use of these resources, such as coal and oil, it is hard to imagine how Western economies could have developed so much, and created such wealth and prosperity over the past centuries.

Clearly however, this development has come at a cost. A plethora of studies have shown a link between the burning of fossil fuels and global warming. Some have claimed that man-made climate change may even be responsible for greater volatility in global weather systems, contributing for example to more severe hurricanes, such as Katrina, which ripped apart New Orleans in 2005. Others have predicted that, should global temperatures continue to increase, within decades the polar icecaps could melt, potentially raising sea levels around the world and flooding major cities, including New York and London. Further feared outcomes include the shutdown of the Gulf Stream across the Atlantic, which some claim could seriously disrupt the climate in northern Europe and further afield.

timeline

1992	1997
Earth summit in Rio de Janeiro calls for governments to stabilize greenhouse gas levels	Kyoto Treaty negotiated – countries agree to bring their emissions under control

> ❝The evidence on the seriousness of the risks from inaction or delayed action is now overwhelming. We risk damages on a scale larger than the two world wars of the last century. The problem is global and the response must be a collaboration on a global scale.❞
>
> Sir Nicholas Stern, UK economist

The environmental dilemma Such eventualities would be disastrous for the world's future prosperity, and so we face a major dilemma. Should we cut back on our current consumption of fossil fuels to lessen the impact that climate change may have on future generations, even though this will mean weaker growth and greater poverty in the immediate future? Or should we continue as we are, assuming that tomorrow's generation, being richer and further advanced scientifically, will discover a way of combating or mitigating climate change?

According to Sir Nicholas Stern, a UK economist who authored one of the first reports on the dilemma, the eventual costs associated with climate change could mount to around 20 per cent of global gross domestic product – around $6 trillion – compared with costs of just 1 per cent of GDP to tackle the threat now.

However, the alternative option of waiting should not be dismissed out of hand. Throughout history, technological advances have helped solve apparently intractable environmental issues. One has only to consider the apocalyptic forecasts of Thomas Malthus compared to the eventual, rather more happy, outcome, to realize that the market tends to develop solutions to the problems it faces.

For example, during Victorian times in London, one of the main fears of the population was the concern that as the city grew, and with it the

2005
EU emissions trading scheme goes into operation

2007
Western economies agree to halve global CO_2 emissions by 2050

number of horses on the streets, the English capital would eventually become buried in a pile of horse manure. Of course, such an outcome never transpired because of the birth of the motor car (which, of course, has its own environmental issues). Similarly, there is much evidence to suggest that new technologies – whether hydrogen-powered motor cars, nuclear-fusion generators or carbon-capture facilities to allow clean burning of coal – will help solve the crisis without subtracting significant economic growth from today's generation.

The greatest externality Climate change is an example of market failure. In the words of Sir Nicholas Stern, it is the worst market failure the world has ever seen. In a properly functioning market, the price of something goes up when its supply falls or demand for it rises – this is a key element of the invisible hand theory propounded by Adam Smith (see chapter 1). If everyone is selfish, markets will produce what people want and the greater good is served.

However, because until very recently there was no price put on either fresh air or pollution, no one in the economy took much notice of them. No one 'owns' the environment in the strictest sense, although of course all humans do. This is what economists call an externality. The actual implied cost of pollution is very high. If pollution causes more hurricanes, more desertification and higher sea levels, and lays waste to towns and cities, it will come at a great price. But it is only since scientists realized the potential of climate change for unleashing such phenomena that work has been done to work out the true cost. In theory, the price of combating climate change ought to be what people are willing to pay in order to ensure that they and their children have clean air in the future. If they are prepared to put up with polluted air and all its consequences, there is no externality.

How countries can cut their emissions

1. Green taxes. Levies on activities that pollute the atmosphere, including taxes on fuels, on power companies for the carbon they produce, and on the dumping of hazardous materials.

2. Carbon trading. This is the preferred economists' method and involves governments auctioning permits to companies allowing them to emit a certain amount of carbon. It thus puts a price on CO_2 emissions. Any company needing to pollute more can then buy a permit off one needing to pollute less, the total amount of emissions being controlled. The problem with this scheme is that carbon trading is still in its infancy, and has until recently been regarded with suspicion by most nations outside the European Union.

3. Technology. Various green technologies, ranging from solar energy to electric-powered cars, could cut emissions. The obstacle is that, until recently, such technologies have been more expensive than simply burning coal or oil. However, as more is invested in them, they are likely to become more affordable.

The challenge Scientists have argued that by 2050, in order to prevent catastrophic effects from climate change, the world must reduce by half its greenhouse emissions (so called because they cause heat to be trapped in the earth's atmosphere, as in a greenhouse). They have called for action to combat deforestation, which is responsible for increasing global greenhouse gas emissions by 15–20 per cent.

Such targets are extremely tough to meet – because not everyone in the world accepts they need to be met. For some years the US and a number of other countries, including Australia and China, repeatedly refrained from committing to global emissions reduction pledges for fear of damaging their economies. A cut in greenhouse gases usually goes hand in hand with weaker growth.

Furthermore, developing nations such as China, Brazil and India have argued, with some justification, that they should not bear the responsibility of cutting their emissions significantly. As climate change is largely a result of pollution generated by the Western world – not these younger economies – why should they have to pay for others' mess? Unfortunately, it is precisely these younger economies that are set to generate the vast majority of extra pollution in the coming years. Similarly, it is the poorest countries – particularly those located in the tropics – that are likely to be worst affected by climate change.

It should also be acknowledged that, although the weight of scientific opinion suggests that global warming is both real and man-made, some remain sceptical about the evidence. However, the dominant view is that the cost of inaction (tomorrow's potential climate disaster) is far greater than the cost of acting now (restraining emissions and economic growth). Combating climate change should, as such, be viewed as an insurance policy for future generations.

the condensed idea
Act now to avoid terrible environmental costs

46 Behavioural economics

Economics has an Achilles' heel. Until recently many practitioners attempted to ignore or dispute this shortcoming – but it can ultimately be held responsible for many of the glaring mistakes economists have made for hundreds of years. It is the erroneous assumption that humans are rational.

Experience shows that people are by no means consistently rational. An obese smoker, were he truly rational, would go on an immediate diet and give up cigarettes, recognizing the danger he is causing to his health. Were each of us truly rational, we wouldn't be so swayed by 'buy one get one free offers'; we would judge the adequacy of our salaries based entirely on their absolute level rather than comparing them to what our neighbour, or our spouse's sister's husband, earned.

Yet, despite these commonplace examples of irrationality, standard 'neoclassical' economics hinges on the notion that people have a limitless capacity for rationality, willpower and selfishness. It is the foundation of Adam Smith's invisible hand theory (see chapter 1), which posited that when selfish, rational actions take place en masse, it will result, overall, in a more prosperous society. This typical rational man imagined by economists is often dubbed *Homo economicus*.

In reality, however, people are prone to emotion – to excitement, love, jealousy and grief, for example – which can make them act irrationally.

timeline

1955	1970s
Nobel Prize-winner Herbert Simon questions the assumption that people have unlimited information-processing capabilities	Tversky and Kahneman pioneer combining psychology and economics

The origins Behavioural economics investigates why and how people act irrationally. It is among the newest and most fascinating areas of academic study, combining economics and psychology. Moreover, far from merely being an interesting realm of study, it is now starting to play a key role in economic policymaking. And as understanding develops as to how the mind and the brain work, so behavioural economists are providing greater insight into what really drives people to act as they do.

The pioneers of behavioural economics were psychologists Amos Tversky and Daniel Kahneman, who, in the 1970s, adapted theories on how the brain processes information and compared them with economic models.

They found that when people are faced with uncertainty, they tend to react neither rationally nor indeed randomly but in certain predictable

Five principles of behavioural economics

1. People are swayed by moral and value judgements. They often do what they believe is 'right' rather than what would gain them most profit.

2. People apply quite different judgements to situations where money is or isn't involved. They distinguish between these market and social contexts. To a neoclassical economist, however, it makes no odds whether you give your best friend a book worth $20 for Christmas or a $20 bill.

3. People are irrational financial investors. They put more weight on recent events than far-off ones, and are not particularly good at calculating probabilities. Similarly, they don't react very well to losing cash. They are prone to hang on to investments since they have a strong sense of possession.

4. People often follow their habits rather than examining their behaviour to see whether it is optimal. Old habits die hard.

5. People are an amalgam of experiences – theirs and other people's. They often do things by observing others rather than because of their own individual judgement.

1980
Behavioural economics starts to influence theories of savings

1996
Amos Tversky dies

2002
Daniel Kahneman awarded the Nobel Prize in Economics

> **Without doubt, the next hot research topic [is] behavioural economics, which integrates economics and psychology. [It] has promise for providing new perspective on public policy.**
>
> Greg Mankiw, Harvard economics professor

ways. Typically, they use mental shortcuts – rules of thumb – which Tversky and Kahneman called *heuristics*. These can be influenced by experience or environment. For instance, someone who has been burnt by a frying pan will tend to be more careful when picking one up in the future.

The evidence People can also be influenced into taking particular decisions by the way a certain proposition is described to them – something known as *framing*. For instance, in one paper Tversky and Kahneman laid out the scenario that the US was facing the outbreak of an unusual Asian disease expected to kill 600 people. They posited two alternative courses of action: Program A in which a projected 200 people will be saved, and Program B, which has a one-third probability that 600 people will be saved and a two-thirds probability that no one will be saved. Some 72 per cent of respondents chose Program A, although the actual outcomes of the two programmes are identical.

A more recent example comes from MIT behavioural economist Dan Ariely, who asked his students to write part of their Social Security number on a piece of paper, and then to suggest how much they would be willing to pay for a bottle of wine. The amount they were prepared to pay depended on their Social Security number – those with the lowest digits tended to bid the lowest and those with the highest bid more. This phenomenon is known as *anchoring*, and, like framing, it undermines the firmly held view that prices in the marketplace are a function of supply and demand.

The latest development in behavioural economics capitalizes on modern MRI technology to scan subjects' brains and link the activity observed to economic decisions. One interesting finding from *neuroeconomics* is that when someone trying to sell something is offered an insulting price by a potential buyer, the part of the brain that reacts is the same that activates when people encounter a disgusting smell or image.

Nudge economics So people do not always make decisions based on their own self-interest. This is a profoundly important realization, since most economies are structured largely on such an assumption. For instance, economists usually assume that people will save throughout their lives because it is in their own interests to have money left over for when they retire. They assume that people will not take on more debt than they believe they can reasonably handle. In fact, according to behavioural economics, we are quite often pushed into taking on debt not by self-interest but by heuristics. The powerful implication is that people need to be nudged in a certain direction – to save, to lose weight, to improve their finances – rather than being expected to do it of their own volition.

This has led to what some call 'libertarian paternalism' or 'nudge economics' – efforts to put behavioural economics into practice. For instance, although people should not be deprived of free choice, some argue they should be pushed gently in a particular, positive direction. A commonplace example is that of automatically enrolling employees in a pension scheme but offering them an opt-out. Another controversial idea – mooted by UK Prime Minister Gordon Brown in 2008 – is to apply this idea of 'presumed consent' to organ donations, assuming by default that everyone is willing to be a donor unless they explicitly indicate otherwise.

However, such schemes clearly can be dangerous in the wrong hands. Governments have a duty to ensure their citizens are protected from war, crime and penury, but should they also be protected from their own irrationality? Where would such discretion stop? If people make the wrong decisions on savings, or on organ donation, might they not make the wrong decision in the polling booth?

Notwithstanding these concerns, the field of economics has been transformed by behavioural insights, which have irrevocably undermined the assumption that humans always act rationally and in their own self-interest. The truth is that people are more complex. For the economics of tomorrow, the task is to find a way to integrate these two models.

the condensed idea
People are predictably irrational

47 Game theory

A scene from the classic 1987 film *The Princess Bride*, adapted from the William Golding book, pitches the hero Westley against his foe Vizzini in a battle of wits. Westley places two glasses of wine on the table and says he has added a deadly poison called iocane powder into one of them. He challenges Vizzini to pick a glass.

'But it's so simple,' says Vizzini. He continues:

> All I have to do is divine from what I know of you. Are you the sort of man who would put the poison into his own goblet, or his enemy's? Now, a clever man would put the poison into his own goblet, because he would know that only a great fool would reach for what he was given. I'm not a great fool, so I can clearly not choose the wine in front of you. But you must have known I was not a great fool; you would have counted on it, so I can clearly not choose the wine in front of me.

Eventually they drink, Vizzini from his glass and Westley from his, whereupon Westley warns Vizzini he chose poorly. Vizzini who has secretly switched the goblets just laughs with glee.

As it happens, Westley has actually poisoned both glasses, having built up an immunity to iocane powder, so Vizzini keels over while the hero rescues the Princess Buttercup. The film doesn't on the face of it seem to have much to do with economics. But what we have just considered is a perfect example of game theory.

Game theory is the science behind human strategy. It is the study of how humans attempt to second-guess each other's actions, and what the

timeline

1944	1950
The Theory of Games and Economic Behavior by John von Neumann and Oskar Morgenstein is published	Prisoner's Dilemma formulated; Nash proposes his theory of equilibrium

ultimate consequences will be. As such, it has become one of the most influential economics ideas of recent decades. Adam Smith argued in the 18th century that humans are inherently selfish, but that when this selfishness is channelled through a market, the end result will be to make society better-off. Game theory, by contrast, examines how people's selfishness informs the way they bargain with each other.

The prisoner's dilemma The classic model of game theory posits a prison, where two accomplices to a crime are interviewed separately from each other. They have two options: either confess to the crime or stay silent. If one confesses and his partner in crime stays silent, the confessor will be given a complete acquittal, while his accomplice will face a jail term of ten years. If both stay silent they will each receive a token one-year sentence. If both confess they will be imprisoned for five years.

The mathematics indicates that the most sensible option for both would be to stay silent. However, one of the precepts of game theory is that individuals' selfishness means they will invariably both betray each other, since the incentive to avoid the longest jail sentence, plus the chance of getting off for free, are more compelling than taking the gamble of remaining silent and being betrayed by one's accomplice. The point is that in certain circumstances the best decision is not always the obvious one.

What, though, if the prisoner's dilemma is repeated over and over again? In such circumstances, where the prisoners know the parameters of the game, they can learn that cooperation is more beneficial a tactic than betrayal. Similarly, when this dilemma has been used as an experiment, it has occasionally highlighted people's propensity to choose the altruistic path of remaining silent.

Another example of game theory is to be found in the James Dean classic movie *Rebel Without a Cause*, where the protagonist takes on an opponent in a game of 'chicken', in which they race cars towards a cliff – the loser

> ‘Do not do unto others as you would have them do unto you. Their tastes may be different.’
> George Bernard Shaw

1960	1982	1994
The Strategy of Conflict by Thomas Schelling is published	Maynard Smith publishes *Evolution and the Theory of Games*	Nash receives the Nobel Prize for Economics

Hollywood meets game theory

Game theory found an unlikely popular audience when it featured in the Oscar-winning 2001 film *A Beautiful Mind*. Russell Crowe portrayed one of its earliest theorists – mathematician John Nash – who suffered paranoid schizophrenia for much of his career, before winning the Nobel Prize for Economics in 1994. However, Nash's achievement was not in devising game theory – the theory's original pioneer was Princeton mathematician John von Neumann – but in refining and finding applications for it. The Nash equilibrium – the theory that Nash devised – describes the situation when two players in a game know what their opponent's strategy is but, unsure about whether their opponent will change his or her mind, they each choose nonetheless to stick to the same strategy.

being the first to jump out of his speeding car. Although they are seeking the best outcome for themselves, they risk the worst – their own death.

The art of second-guessing However, game theory is a much broader study than such examples suggest. It examines how humans behave in any 'game-like' scenario – as opposed to those where no strategy is involved. What these scenarios have in common is that the actions of one participant invariably influence the outcome not only for themselves but for others. This can include zero-sum games where the interests of each participant clash such that one person's win is another's loss, or games with a win-win outcome.

Key to the theory is the fact that in such circumstances people are forced to second-guess another rational, self-interested human's intentions. Given how widely strategic interdependence applies to human interaction, game theory has become an extremely influential and frequently applied discipline, used in politics, economics and commerce. Bankers employ it when working on takeovers, employers and trades unions when engaged in wage disputes, politicians when negotiating, for example, on international trade agreements – or most controversially, when considering whether or not to go to war – and companies use it when determining how to price their products and outsell their rivals.

War games One of the earliest and most controversial applications of game theory was during the Cold War. Both the Soviet Union and the US had nuclear weapons capable of causing massive devastation to each other's countries; both knew that to fire one would result in mutually assured destruction; in other words, that their opponent would launch missiles in response. Indeed, philosopher Bertrand Russell likened the nuclear stand-off to a game of chicken.

In his classic 1960 book *The Strategy of Conflict*, Thomas Schelling explored how game theory would motivate the Soviet Union and the US to respond to each other. One of his striking conclusions was that countries facing such a stand-off would be better placed attempting to protect their weapons rather than their people. The rationale is that a country that believed it could withstand the consequences of nuclear war would be the most likely to start one. So, said Schelling, rather than building nuclear shelters for everybody, it would be better to demonstrate your ability to strike back with force if your opponent should launch a warhead in your direction. Such insights influenced the way the Cold War opponents approached the art of brinkmanship – persuading them, for instance, to put warheads in submarines rather than just in static land sites. The problem, in this case, was that neither side knew how many missiles the other had nor where they were located or aimed, but such uncertainty only perpetuated the stand-off.

Science or art A classic game theory experiment is one most of us have played: chess. Whenever we play strategic games we take decisions based on what we anticipate our opponent will do. The number of possible moves at any one stage of the game, however, is almost infinite, so there is little option but to think a few moves ahead and rely on both experience and intuition to fill in the rest of the gaps.

Game theory remains one of the most fast-developing areas of economics, and is increasingly helping to uncover fundamental truths about human behaviour. However, in the words of one of its leading experts, Avinash Dixit of Princeton University, 'The theory is far from complete, and in many ways the design of successful strategy remains an art.'

the condensed idea
People behave differently in games

48 Criminomics

What happens when economics is shifted outside the boardroom and into the bedroom; when it is used to examine criminals rather than companies? What transpires when its tools are transplanted to studying everything from the black market to family life? So powerful and universal are the tools of economic theory – from supply and demand to game theory – that they can be used to shed light on all sorts of apparently unconnected issues.

Consider the parable of the bagel seller – one of many examples set out by Steven Levitt and Stephen Dubner in their 2005 book *Freakonomics* (based on economics professor Levitt's research). It goes something like this: an entrepreneur who delivers bagels to companies decides that, rather than hanging around and waiting for each customer to pay him in turn, he will simply leave behind a cash box and a note asking them to pay what they owe. Reassuringly, he does pretty well out of this honour system. And, more interestingly, his accounts unearth some fascinating trends: for instance, people are more honest when they work in smaller offices, when the weather is good, and when a holiday is round the corner.

The book comes up with unconventional conclusions about some of modern society's most contentious issues – abortion and race for instance. Among other things, it reveals surprising links between the Ku Klux Klan and estate agents, as well as uncovering the cheating habits of Chicago school teachers and sumo wrestlers.

The point, however, is that even in the most offbeat, non-market-related environments, the fundamental rules of economics can apply – whether this means supply and demand, the invisible hand, human incentives or

timeline

1776

The Wealth of Nations by Adam Smith is published

Parenthood: altruism or investment?

Parents often treat their children with apparent altruism. They shower them with attention and gifts for very little direct reward, doing so in spite of the fact that babies are inherently selfish for much of their childhood. While many assume this is merely a manifestation of familial love, Becker argues otherwise. He claims that the parents' indulgence is instead a means of investing indirectly for their own old age. The rate of return, he argues, from investing in one's children exceeds that of regular retirement savings, since a successful and wealthy child is likely to look after his or her parents if need be.

any other parts of the pantheon of economic rules. After all, economics is the study of human decision-making, which does not necessarily need a money-oriented backdrop against which to function.

However, Levitt and Dubner's book, which was highly successful and spawned a number of imitators in the following years, did not represent the first time a trained economist applied these rules to normal everyday life. The real pioneer of such an approach was Gary Becker, an economist at the University of Chicago. Becker, who was awarded the Nobel Prize in 1992, showed that everyone – from criminals to racists to families to drug addicts – is in some way influenced by economic forces such as rational decision-making and incentives.

Getting away with it At the heart of Becker's theories and arguments is the idea that there is almost always a cost attached to something – even if it is a social or emotional cost as opposed to an explicit sum of money. For instance, one of his ideas is that those who discriminate against minorities will often mentally increase the cost of a transaction if it involves interacting with them.

> **'Since the science of economics is primarily a set of tools, as opposed to a subject matter, then no subject, however offbeat, need be beyond its reach.'**
>
> **Steven Levitt**

1992
Gary Becker wins the
Nobel Prize for Economics

2003
Steven Levitt wins the John
Bates Clark Medal

2005
Freakonomics is published

> ❝The amount of crime is determined not only by the rationality and preferences of would-be criminals, but also by the economic and social environment created by public policies, including expenditures on police, punishments for different crimes, and opportunities for employment, schooling, and training programs.❞
>
> Gary Becker

Gary Becker's Eureka moment came when he found himself having to decide between parking in an illegal spot or driving to a designated car park a few blocks away at the cost of his extra time and effort. He opted for the illegal spot, judging that the risk of being caught and punished did not outweigh the extra effort of having to drive the car to the further spot and walk all the way back again. Similar judgements, he concluded, were taken by criminals in deciding whether to break the law.

The conclusion has important implications for how politicians run their justice systems, since it supports the idea that fines and penalties should be more severe. The tougher the penalty, the greater the cost of getting caught and the greater the deterrent. It was this insight which helped Becker towards his Nobel Prize.

The theory was proven some years later by Levitt, who compared juvenile crime rates in various US states and compared them with the crime rates for adults. He found that as soon as these criminals became old enough to face the far harsher sentences meted out to adults their criminal activity tended to become less frequent.

Indeed, Tim Harford, the author of *The Undercover Economist*, saw this firsthand when he was driven by Becker to a restaurant, where the Nobel Prize-winner parked in a bay with a 30-minute time limit, which he far exceeded. Since the bays were not checked too often, he judged the risk of being caught worth taking, given the convenience of the location. He did it all the time, he said, and while he occasionally got fined it was never so frequent as to deter him from parking there. He was merely behaving rationally.

Social applications Economics, of course, does not just apply to criminal situations. Harford, for example, has shown that those in speed-dating sessions tend to raise or lower their expectations for the quality of mate they are seeking based not on their absolute demands but on the quality of the field they encounter. The number of people who successfully select tends to remain constant, regardless of whether the field is devastatingly attractive or not. This is, essentially, a lesson in anchoring – one of the precepts of behavioural economics (see chapter 46).

Levitt uses economic theories to prove that children are defined less by the way they are brought up than by their parents' economic and often ethnic background. He also famously argued that the reason US crime rates dropped in the 1990s was because the legalization of abortion in the 1970s meant families in deprived areas no longer reproduced uncontrollably.

'Macroeconomics isn't really about human behaviour,' says Levitt:

> Economics is one of a set of broad tools for looking at the world. But it tells you to put in place policies that are absurd, because it doesn't worry about things like fairness or morality, or psychological factors.

> In economics, the right punishment for parking in a handicapped parking spot would be execution with a very low frequency, or torture with a very low frequency – and I think that would be completely reasonable.

While there are limits as to the applicability of economic theories to everyday life, there is also a clear lesson for policymakers: economics is not a perfect framework for viewing the world. However, it is the best method available for determining how to influence people and how to predict their behaviour. And that goes just as equally for our social peccadilloes as it does for our financial trials and tribulations. It is a conclusion Adam Smith would have heartily approved of.

the condensed idea
Economics can apply
to everything

49 Happynomics

In the 1970s, in the tiny Himalayan kingdom of Bhutan, the country's economy was coming under major scrutiny. By most measures – gross domestic product, national income, employment and so on, it was growing sluggishly. So the King of Bhutan did something unusual. He decreed that from then on Bhutan's progress would be measured not against these traditional economic yardsticks but against its Gross National Happiness.

It might have seemed an unconventional response to outside criticism, but the king had struck upon an idea that would grow into an important, increasingly respectable study – that of happiness economics. It is a subject most of us can relate to. As nations and individuals, almost all of us are richer and healthier than ever before. However, this wealth has gone hand in hand with a malaise of discontent. Those in rich nations have been getting less and less happy over the past 50 years.

The pursuit of happiness Traditional economics does not have a satisfactory explanation for this. Since the time of Adam Smith, wealth has been assumed to be the key measure of a country's progress. It is for this reason – and the fact that money is easy to measure – that economists have tended to concentrate on measures such as gross domestic product, unemployment and a handful of other social measures such as life expectancy and inequality. But not, until recently, happiness, which, given how much importance philosophers have placed on contentedness since the earliest days of humanity, is somewhat surprising.

timeline

1776	1780
The US Declaration of Independence asserts the right to 'life, liberty and the pursuit of happiness'	Jeremy Bentham devises the 'greatest happiness principle'

The idea that a country's progress should be measured against its happiness did not, in fact, begin in Bhutan twenty or so years ago. In 1776 Thomas Jefferson laid down that Americans should be entitled not just to life and liberty but to 'the pursuit of happiness'. Jeremy Bentham, the 19th-century inventor of the philosophy of utilitarianism, said that humans should strive for the 'greatest happiness of the greatest number'.

Pursuing happiness seems to have yielded definite results in Bhutan. Since taking up the gross national happiness index, the country has grown at a remarkable rate by even conventional economic terms. In 2007 it was the second-fastest growing economy in the world, all the while managing to increase its gross national happiness. In an effort to sustain people's contentedness, there have been decrees that 60 per cent of the country should remain covered in forest, while tourism, which apparently undermines happiness, is capped each year. Money is redistributed from rich to poor so as to help eliminate mass poverty.

Measuring happiness These efforts to make Bhutan happier seem to have borne rich fruit. According to a survey in 2005, only 3 per cent of people reported not being happy, while almost half the population said they were very happy. But such surveys can often be vague, unconvincing

The hierarchy of needs

There are some basic human needs, all of which ought to be fulfilled if we are to be happy. They range from the physiological (one's bodily functions working properly) and safety (shelter, employment, health) to love, esteem and morality. This hierarchy, devised by psychologist Abraham Maslow in a 1943 paper, underpins what contributes to human contentedness. Happiness economists have found that once the most basic needs – those of physiology and safety – are met, one's happiness can often diminish.

1972

Bhutan starts to develop a gross national happiness index

2006

After a military coup in Thailand the new prime minister Surayud Chulanont sets up a similar index

> ❝The ideology of Gross National Happiness connects Bhutan's development goals with the pursuit of happiness. This means that the ideology reflects Bhutan's vision on the purpose of human life, a vision that puts the individual's self-cultivation at the centre.❞
>
> **Dasho Meghraj Gurung, Bhutan minister**

and difficult to compare empirically. Happiness is far more difficult to measure than, for instance, levels of wealth or life expectancy, and it is this that has caused its neglect in economics. However, recent advances in brain scans have helped neuroscientists identify which part of the central nervous system is most stimulated by happiness, and the findings have helped add a layer of scientific credibility to measures of happiness.

In recent decades, economists and psychologists have, for the first time, started measuring, in earnest, people's happiness in long-term studies. The conclusion they have come to is that although one's happiness increases as one goes from being poor to rich, the level of contentedness starts to drop off as one gets further from the poverty line. According to Richard Layard, a British economist who specializes in happiness economics, once a nation's average salary goes beyond $20,000, income rises stop making people happier and gradually make them less content. In economic phraseology, there are diminishing returns of happiness beyond that point.

This is what Richard Easterlin, one of the pioneers of the study, calls a 'hedonic cycle' (from the ancient Greek word for pleasure): once you get rich you get accustomed to it very quickly, and soon take such a standard of life for granted. Moreover, research from the field of behavioural economics (see chapter 46) has shown that once one's basic needs are fulfilled we start to measure our own contentedness based not on our absolute wealth or achievements, but in comparison to others. The old adage that one is happy with one's salary provided it is higher than one's wife's sister's husband's has a definite basis in psychology. Such findings indicate that a 24-hour-news-and-celebrity culture, with the lifestyles of the rich, beautiful and famous constantly advertised, is likely to undermine people's contentedness yet further.

Money isn't everything Ministers everywhere from the UK, Australia, China and Thailand are engaged on a quest to determine an internationally comparable measure of gross national well-being. While some traditional economists deride such objectives, it would be wrong to assume that the current palette of measures on a country's progress are definitive. One independent measure, devised by the New Economics Foundation, is the Happy Planet Index, which combines measures of a country's life satisfaction, life expectancy and ecological footprint per capita. According to this, the best-scoring country in the world in 2006 was the Pacific island of Vanuatu, followed by Colombia and Costa Rica, while Burundi, Swaziland and Zimbabwe were the worst. The majority of the world's richest countries, including the US and UK, came more than halfway down the list.

Happiness economics is increasingly influencing the way politicians in developed countries create policy. It has been suggested, for example, that higher taxes on big earners will make society as a whole happier, since they will reduce national levels of envy. Another idea is that companies should limit the extent to which workers' pay is based on merit. Lord Layard has suggested funding mass programmes of cognitive behavioural therapy for all members of the population. Although such ideas are controversial, they are rapidly gaining traction in the UK and the US, as politicians seek a way to inspire apathetic voters.

The growth of happiness economics has inspired a mild backlash. Some psychologists have argued that discontent and envy can play an important role in driving people to better themselves. And then there's the question of whether pursuing a nation's happiness is entirely morally sound. In 1990, Bhutan expelled 100,000 ethnic outsiders from the country. The move reportedly boosted national happiness but at the cost of undermining its human rights record. Wealth is clearly not everything, but then neither is happiness.

the condensed idea
Economics is not all about money

50 21st-century economics

Economists have been derided for failing to foresee major shifts in the financial landscape and missing clues that pointed to a sudden stock market catastrophe. But now, in the early years of the third millennium, more fundamental questions have been raised about the foundations of the subject – these ones too difficult to dismiss.

First is the fact that its key doctrines, laid down first by John Maynard Keynes and then Milton Friedman, were tried to destruction in the 20th century, often with unhappy results.

Second is a more fundamental failing. Since the subject's very earliest days, economics has more or less relied on the idea that humans act rationally: that they always act in their own self-interest, and that such actions, in a fully functioning market, will make society better off (see chapter 1).

However, this does not explain why people frequently take decisions that are ostensibly not in their own interests. It is in no one's self-interest to send themselves to an early grave, but despite widespread knowledge about the dangers of lung cancer and obesity, people still smoke and eat fatty foods. Similar arguments have been levied against climate change and man-made pollution.

New disciplines such as behavioural economics (see chapter 46) have revealed that much of the time people take decisions based not on what would be best for them but on so-called heuristics – rules of thumb from their own experience – or by copying others.

timeline

1776	1930s
The Wealth of Nations by Adam Smith is published	Great Depression ushers in Keynesian policies

Mortgage malaise

Conventional economics assumes that people can skilfully select the best product for their interests despite the complexity of the task. That this was a flawed assumption was proven as housing markets boomed in the early 2000s. Many less well-off families took out mortgages not realizing that, after a few years of cheap interest rates, their monthly repayments would suddenly shoot up to unaffordable levels. Conventional economists did not foresee the scale of the subsequent crash in part because they failed to appreciate that people were taking apparently irrational decisions which would ultimately cause them to lose their home.

A pick and mix approach In the light of the realization that people don't always act rationally, regulators are likely to become more paternalistic in the future. There are, for example, already attempts to regulate the mortgage market more stringently so that it is less easy for consumers to make choices against their best long-term interest.

Economics is evolving from a subject that placed an almost limitless amount of faith in the ability of markets to determine outcomes to one that questions whether markets always come up with the preferred outcome. Rather like the modern novel, which picks and chooses from a variety of different styles instead of limiting itself to one discourse, 21st-century economics will pick and choose widely from Keynesianism, monetarism, rational market theory and behavioural economics to come up with a new fusion.

the condensed idea
Intervene when people are not rational

early 1980s	1990s	2000s
Monetarist ideas are implemented by Ronald Reagan and Margaret Thatcher	Behavioural economics gains popularity	A new fusion of economics starts to gain favour

Glossary

Absolute advantage When a country can produce something more efficiently, in other words at less expense and effort, than another.

Aggregate Another word for 'total'. Refers to a big figure – for example, gross domestic product or a company's total sales over a year.

Automatic stabilizers A government's expenditure or receipts, which expand or contract to compensate for the economy's booms and busts.

Bank run When fearful customers all try simultaneously to pull their savings out of a bank, often leading to its collapse.

Bear market When there is a steady drop in the stock market, which leads to widespread pessimism and downward growth.

Bond A certificate of debt from a country, state or company.

Bull market When there is investor confidence, which leads to widespread optimism and upward growth.

Capital Money or physical assets used to produce an income.

Capitalism The economic system in which capital is owned by private individuals and corporations.

Capital controls State-imposed restrictions on the amount of capital allowed in and out of a country.

Capital markets The broad term for markets where equities and bonds are issued and traded.

Central bank The main monetary authority of a country. It issues the national currency and regulates the supply of credit – most notably by controlling interest rates.

Communism The Marxist idea that capitalism would be succeeded by a society in which the people (or rather the government) own the means of production within an economy.

Credit A polite word for debt; a promise to pay someone in the future for what one borrows today.

Credit crunch A financial crisis which makes banks reluctant or unable to lend money, causing the rest of the economy to suffer.

Default When a person, institution or country fails to repay its debts.

Deficit A shortfall in an account – be it a government's budget deficit or an entire country's current account deficit.

Deflation A situation where the prices of goods in an economy are, on average, falling rather than rising.

Demand The total amount of goods or services people are willing and able to buy at a given price. Usually, as the price rises, people demand fewer goods.

Depression A severe recession. Usually defined as a gross domestic product contraction of 10 per cent, or a recession that lasts three years or more.

Employment rate The percentage of the workforce with jobs.

Equilibrium price The price at which the supply of goods matches demand.

Exports Goods and services that are produced domestically and then sold to foreign countries.

Fiscal policy The decisions a government takes about what to spend its money on, how to raise taxes and how much to borrow.

Gold standard An international system in which countries' currencies are fixed in relation to gold prices.

Hedge funds A type of investment vehicle which can bet on a company's value decreasing or increasing, as well as many other more complex strategies.

Hyperinflation When inflation runs out of control. A highly damaging phenomenon most notoriously experienced by Germany in the 1920s and Zimbabwe in the 2000s.

IMF The International Monetary Fund. An international organization charged with monitoring the global economy and rescuing countries facing funding crises.

Imports Goods and services bought from overseas.

Inflation The rate at which the price of goods throughout an economy is increasing.

Interest The amount, expressed in a percentage, that someone can hope to receive back on an investment. Conversely it can be the amount someone is charged for borrowing.

Laissez-faire From the French 'let (them) do (as they choose); where governments try as much as possible to leave the market to its own devices.

Liquidity A measure of how easy it is for someone to exchange an asset – for instance a house, a gold bar or a pack of cigarettes – for money or other types of currency.

Macroeconomics The study of government and international economics: taking a step back and examining how whole economies work and perform – what drives gross domestic product, prices or unemployment.

Marginal The difference it makes to buy or sell one extra unit of something, as opposed to the average cost of a product.

Market Where buyers and sellers meet (often virtually) to trade goods and services.

Microeconomics The study of the minutiae within economies: what makes people take certain decisions, how companies become profitable, and so on.

Monetary policy The decisions a government or central bank (usually the latter) make about regulating the amount and price of money flowing around the economy.

Money Assets commonly used to purchase goods and settle debts. It is a medium of exchange, a unit of account and a store of value.

Money markets The web of dealers and investors in short-term lending – anything from a few hours to a year.

Money supply The amount of money flowing around an economy.

Monopoly The exclusive control by one seller of a particular product in a market.

Negative equity Where someone's asset, usually their home, falls in value so much that it becomes worth less than the mortgage or loan that funded it.

Privatization When a company or institution which was previously government-owned is sold off to a privately owned entity.

Productivity The amount of economic output generated compared with the amount of effort (in terms of hours worked or number of workers).

Quantitative easing Methods central banks employ when interest rates no longer work, as happened in Japan in the 1990s and much of the Western world in the 2000s. It attempts to influence the quantity rather than the price of money in the economy.

Recession A fall in a country's economic fortunes: when GDP contracts rather than grows for two successive quarters.

Securities Financial contracts that grant someone a stake in an asset: this can mean everything from bonds and shares to complex derivatives.

Shares Also known as equities. A unit of ownership in a company. Shares entitle the owner to a dividend, and a right to vote on the company's plans.

Stagflation When high inflation is coupled with stagnant economic growth.

Subsidy A sum of cash given by someone – usually a government – to support a particular business or industry. They are often reviled as a form of protectionism.

Supply The total amount of goods or services which can be bought at a particular price. Together with demand, this is what powers a market economy.

Tariff A fee imposed by a government on goods imported from overseas.

Zero-sum game Where the winner's gains equal the losses of the losers. This contrasts with positive-sum games where both parties can profit to some degree.

Index

For further information and resources, visit
www.edmundconway.com

Edited by Nick Fawcett and Ian Crofton
Designed by Patrick Nugent
Proofread by Ilsa Yardley
Indexed by Patricia Hymans

ISBN 978-1-4351-4740-9

Manufactured in China

2 4 6 8 10 9 7 5 3